Other Books by William Powell Tuck

Facing Grief and Death
The Struggle For Meaning (editor)
Knowing God: Religious Knowledge in the Theology of John Baillie
Our Baptist Tradition
Ministry: An Ecumenical Challenge (editor)
Getting Past the Pain
A Glorious Vision
The Bible As Our Guide For Spiritual Growth (editor)
Authentic Evangelism
The Lord's Prayer Today
The Way for All Seasons
Through the Eyes of a Child
Christmas Is for the Young…Whatever Their Age
Love as a Way of Living
The Compelling Faces of Jesus
The Left Behind Fantasy
The Ten Commandments: Their Meaning Today
Facing Life's Ups and Downs
The Church In Today's World
The Church Under the Cross
Modern Shapers of Baptist Thought in America
The Journey to the Undiscovered Country: What's Beyond Death?
A Pastor Preaching: Toward a Theology of the Proclaimed Word
The Pulpit Ministry of the Pastors of River Road Church, Baptist
(editor)
The Last Words from the Cross
*Lord, I Keep Getting a Busy Signal: Reaching for a Better Spiritual
Connection*
Overcoming Sermon Block: The Preacher's Workshop
*A Revolutionary Gospel: Salvation in the Theology of Walter
Rauschenbusch*

ABOUT *HOLIDAYS, HOLY DAYS, & SPECIAL DAYS*

Any book by Dr. William Tuck would make a fitting gift for your church's minister. This one should be especially welcome, as it is a compilation of Dr. Tuck's special-occasion sermons preached over the years for such holidays as Martin Luther King, Jr., Sunday and Mother's Day. Even if your minister doesn't preach them just as they come from the book, he or she will surely be challenged to produce similarly relevant, moving sermons for those occasions. The illustrations alone are worth a lot. They have a way of "earthing" the sermons, of making them real and available to the average listener. I knew when I met Bill Tuck fifty years ago that he was one of God's very special messengers. This book is the most recent confirmation of that judgment.

Dr. John Killinger

Pastor, seminary professor, and author of *101 Tips for New Ministers* and *101 Tips for Ministers' Spouses and Partners*, among many other books, both fiction and nonfiction.

Bill Tuck always seems to know how to weave the biblical, inspirational, personal, and practical together for maximum impact. In the preface, he writes about how people's minds are focused on special days throughout the year and he never wants to miss an opportunity to address them. He then provides us with model sermons on how to do just that.

Subjects include those you would expect to find plus sermons for Martin Luther King, Jr. Day, Valentine's Day, Commencement Day, Earth Day, Independence Day, Labor Day, and Columbus Day. The material is rich in content, illustrations, and creative ways to address the usual in unusual ways.

Each sermon concludes with a prayer. I found it to be one you would want to pray after hearing the sermon. In fact, after reading the entire series my response was simply, "Amen and amen."

Dr. Ron Higdon

Pastor, and author of *Surviving a Son's Suicide* and *In Changing Times*

Bill Tuck has produced a needed and helpful book for preachers of various denominations. It is unique in that it provides well planned sermons on a variety of topics related to significant liturgical, civil, and family themes. These are not sermon starters. They are complete sermons in manuscript form. As such they offer significant practicality and reflect a level of theological insight often lacking in much modern preaching. Dr. Tuck's sermons are sure to stoke a fire in the hearts of those who read this worthy volume. While a wise preacher will not use these sermons verbatim, as if they were one's own inspiration and creativity, they will surely encourage any preacher to consider a number of potential approaches for preaching these significant occasions.

Sermons on Palm Sunday, Easter, Advent and Christmas are provided from the Church's liturgical calendar. These echo deep appreciation for the shared proclamation of the holy seasons expressed by numerous worship traditions.

The reader will take note of sermons arising from these regularly celebrated holidays: News Year's Day, Mother's Day, Father's Day, Memorial Day, Independence Day, Labor Day, Columbus Day, and Thanksgiving Day. These unique sermons reflect themes that touch the current needs of modern church members.

In addition, three sermons are provided for special days (Valentines, Earth Day, and Commencement) that offer biblical insight into calendared annual events that are often neglected in the pulpit.

Preachers of varied worship traditions will be greatly aided by these inspiring and truly biblical messages. Insight is provided that will encourage preachers in the grand work of gospel proclamation. These sermons are solidly rooted in Scripture and in the contemporary world. They rise up from within God's church and are an offering to God's church.

Lee McGlone, Ph.D.
Pastor, First Baptist Church
Arkadelphia, Arkansas
Editor of *The Minister's Manual*

HOLIDAYS, HOLY DAYS & SPECIAL DAYS

PREACHING THROUGH THE YEAR

WILLIAM POWELL TUCK

Energion Publications
Gonzalez, FL
2015

ISBN 10: 1-63199-220-1
ISBN 13: 978-1-63199-220-9
Library of Congress Control Number: 2015956974

Energion Publications
P. O. Box 841
Gonzalez, FL 32560

energion.com
pubs@energion.com
850-525-3916

To Rand Forder,
Gifted preacher and pastor
and my friend for over forty years

PREFACE

Throughout most of my ministry I have preached on the themes of the major holidays and special occasions as well as the regular holy days in the church year. Since people usually had their minds focused on these special occasions, I hated to miss an opportunity to address them. If a minister follows the Lectionary rigidly, he or she will never preach on the ideas heralded in the national holidays. Even if normally a pastor follows the Lectionary, I believe it would be beneficial for one's congregation for him or her to preach on one of the special holiday themes occasionally. I found that Mother's Day, for example, afforded me an opportunity to preach on themes related to the home and family life when people were already focused on this area. Thanksgiving was an occasion to address our need to reflect on gratitude and acknowledging our responsibility to express our thankfulness for our blessings in life. In similar ways the other holidays presented analogous opportunities.

The sermons presented in this book have been preached over the years in churches where I have served as pastor and as interim pastor. I found the congregations receptive to the special emphases and usually desired copies of the sermons. I have found few sermon books that addressed these themes, which I think is a real loss for pastors. Here is one pastor's attempt to preach on these important themes. Hopefully, they can serve as another pastor's model for the way I utilized these holidays and special days to help the congregation focus more clearly on their deeper meanings. I would like to think that other preachers would create their own sermons on these holiday emphases for their own churches. In my opinion, not to preach on these themes is to miss a valuable opportunity.

I express my appreciation once again to Rand Forder, my friend, who has served as a pastor and has preached on many of these themes, for his proof-reading of my original manuscript. I hope that lay persons as well as ministers will find inspiration in these messages.

TABLE OF CONTENTS

Preface

"Resolves For The New Year"

Psalm 36:1-12
Philippians 3:13-14

On New Year's Eve, I, like many of you, witnessed the descent of the giant crystal ball in Times Square as it slowly dropped at midnight and the beginning of 2015 came in. Of course, I, like you, did that via television. One of the interesting things observed was all the excitement and commotion that was created by the people as they waited for that particular moment—the beginning of the New Year. I have often wondered why it is that we get so excited about the beginning of a new year. In many ways there was not much difference that night than from any other night that we normally have—not much except maybe in the way some folks treated that night. But why did we treat it differently? One of the reasons, of course, is we want the opportunity for a new beginning. Most of us feel like we have "goofed up" bad enough in the past, and we welcome any new opportunity to strive ahead in a different kind of way.

Philosophers have always been excited about the meaning of time and have probed deeply to see if they could understand what time really means. Some have said that it has no meaning. To them, all of life, including the present moments of time which we have, is without purpose or direction. Some, like the ancient Greek philosopher, Plato, have said that the time itself in which you and I live is just a reflections of another greater world. You and I are mere projections or reflection of a greater world that we do not know at all. Philosophers have given us all kinds of interpretations. Some are interesting and some not so interesting. All of us desire to know more fully what time means to us.

One of the ancient legends tells of a riddle that was asked by a monster named Sphinx as people passed by his path. If they could not answer his riddle, he would destroy them in the midst of their pilgrimage. His riddle was this: "What animal is it that in the morning walks on all fours, at noon walks on two legs, but in the evening walks on three legs?" A lot of people died before Oedipus came along and answered the riddle. "The animal," he said, "is man." In his infancy he crawls on all fours. When he becomes an adult at noontime of his life, he walks on two legs. When he comes to the evening of life, he walks on three legs because, then, he needs a cane to lean on to support himself.

A small girl overheard her mother musing, "Where does the time go?" "Why, it goes into everything we do," the child responded. And so it does! Time. All kinds of interesting definitions and philosophies have been given to try to help us understand what time is. When you look at life, some have said that life really is very short. Most of us can remember almost nothing about our childhood years before five. We can recall nothing much of our infancy unless we are hypnotized and it is brought back. For most of us, that period of time is lost to memory, at least to conscious memory. We spend, on the average, one-third of our time sleeping, some more than that, some less.

We spend a good deal of our time eating, and some say that you should not count that as valuable time. I count the time spent in eating very valuable because that sometimes is where the greatest communications may take place between people. Some say you should not count the time people spend at work because a lot of people hate their jobs. If you don't count the time of infancy and early childhood, if you don't count the time when we are sleeping, and if you don't count the time when we work on our jobs, our lives really are short, then. But I think that we must count all of this time. What will we do with it? What have we done with it? And what will we do with whatever remainder of time we have before us?

A Lesson from the Apostle Paul

The Apostle Paul, in writing to the Philippians, gives us, what I think, is a very powerful passage that offers direction on how to live in the new year which lies before us. This particular passage we might call a kind of *hinge* passage, because it tells us something to do with the past and also something to do with the future. Paul reminds us that we are to forget those things which are behind us as we press on toward the goal that is ahead of us. There are at least two dimensions to his message in this passage. There are certain things which we need to forget and there are other things that we need to remember.

Learning to Forget

Forgetting really is a gift that comes to us from God. To be able to forget one's achievements or failures and to rise up with a new sense of direction and purpose in one's life is marvelous good news. Within a lifetime, we can bring into our life an awful lot of mental junk, spiritual refuse, which needs to be rooted out and washed from our lives. There are then some things that we need to forget as we come into this New Year.

Forget Your Resentments

The *first* thing I would suggest is for you and for me to learn to *forget our resentments*. It is astounding how many people poison their lives with secret hatreds and resentments which they have toward other people because of something they may have said or not have said, something they may have done or not have done, or some act they did quickly, harshly or in anger. Down inside us, we now seethe with feelings of hatred and resentment toward that individual. We need to let go of these resentments because they poison our lives. They color our whole perspective on life. Our life has turned sour because we can't let go of our hatreds and grudges. They have dyed our whole perspective. We need a way to cultivate the art of letting go of our resentments. Let the new year provide us with an opportunity of forgiving them or seeking forgiveness and rise up as new men and women. May we forget those things which are behind us and press forward for the opportunities of newness which lie ahead of us.

FORGET YOUR WORRIES

Secondly I would suggest that we *forget our worries*. Now, that is not to say you should never have any concern about tomorrow. Intelligent concern and plans are necessary. We need to make preparations so that we can secure our retirement. We need to deal with our health and many other factors in life wisely and intelligently. But a lot of people have needless worry that nags at them, cripples them, and crushes them down to the ground. Jesus never said that we are not supposed to make any plans for the future or prepare for tomorrow. Jesus talked about the foolish virgins who made no preparations for the coming of the bridegroom. He also spoke about a builder taking care to prepare for his construction. So we need to take care and prepare. But needless worry about things over which we have no control only festers at us and brings about inner destruction.

I like the comment of the old, uneducated preacher who said that his favorite verse of scripture in the Bible was "It came to pass." Nothing came to stay. It all came to pass. That may not be good exegesis but it is a valid reflection on life. Whatever we have experienced, even difficulties, they came to pass. Even if there are joys, they came to pass. Whatever is here is for the moment. So we learn from that experience and, then, we move on. To focus in one's life on worry is to live without a sense of the companionship of God. Constant worry as one's companionship is really a disguised kind of atheism, because it is an affirmation that we really do not believe in the providence, care, and presence of God to direct us and guide us. So, let us forget about our worries and put them in the past and focus intelligently on the tomorrows that are ahead of us.

FORGET YOUR PRIVILEGES

We could also learn to *forget about our privileges*. There are too many people that focus their life on "what it has to offer me." What is life going to do for me? If this is our perspective, we see ourselves as privileged persons who always want everybody and everything to give us the advantage or exemption. Instead of focusing on what life owes us we need to turn it around and see what you and I can do to care for the needs of other people. The Apostle Paul did not flaunt his Jewish past and the privileges he had known, but he put that behind him and moved on to the future before him. Is it not more Christian to be concerned with what are the needs of others than always seeking to see if I can not have my needs or my desires satisfied? The higher, more Christian way is to seek to serve. We reach out to our brother or our sister, who may have a deeper need, and seek to meet that need in a sacrificial, loving way. That indeed, I think, is more Christ-like than always desiring that I get special treatment or attention.

FORGET ABOUT FAILURES

I would say we also need to learn to *forget about our failures*. The Apostle Paul was no stranger to failure. He felt he had failed when he started persecuting the Christians, thinking that they were against God. He saw the Christians at first as people who were going to destroy what God was seeking to do in the world. He had failed to see God at work in them. He had known failure. He had known failure even in trying to spread the message of Christ. He had been beaten, stoned, and driven out of towns. He had been rejected, imprisoned, and ridiculed, but he continued on unafraid to share the gospel message.

None of us is a stranger to failure. Each of us in his or her experience has known some kind of failure. Who has not failed a test? Who has not failed to receive some recognition or promotion? Who at some time or another has not lost an opportunity or a job or something else important? We all know something of having to live with difficulties and failures. But as Christians we do not let these crush us down. We seek to put those behind us and move toward what tomorrow will give us. One of the sad things is that so many people focus their lives only on their difficulties, failures and lost opportunities and not on the newness of life which lies before them, and what they can be, do, and become.

Sören Kierkegaard, a Danish philosopher, tells a story about a man who bought some champion horses from the king's coachman. He bought these beautiful stallions wanting to have them as his own horses to show them off and to use with his carriage. He fed them and took care of them, but over a short period of time he noticed that the horses began to lose their great sense of showmanship which once they had had. Their champion appearance soon began to leave them. They began to get thin and did not eat properly. He couldn't understand it, so he called in the king's coachman. The coachman worked with the animals for one month. Then one could see the horses' heads held high and proud once again. Their coats gleamed, their weight was right and they moved with the proper gait. The man asked: "What did you do?" The coachman responded: "I brought the horses up to my expectations and not up to their own expectations."

Too many of us let our failures and defeats give us our perspective on life and that dominates our expectation. God is seeking to call us to be more than we have ever become and to realize the greater possibility of what you and I can be and do as His children in His kingdom.

Forget Your Victories

I think we also need to learn to *forget our victories and our achievements.* Sometimes we assess our worth too much on our achievements. We measure our life by whether or not we are listed in Who's Who or whether we have a trophy chest filled, or a scrapbook filled with all kinds of recognitions, or whether we are listed in the Dunn and Bradstreet ratings. Sometimes we focus too much on thinking that we have arrived and we look too much on our own achievements and forget the power, grace, and ministry of God and what we are because of his grace, love and power. Too often we embrace our achievements as though they were all by our own doing alone.

Paul reminds us in this passage that for Christ's sake he counted all of his former gains as loss. He counted all of them as "garbage." The figure of "refuse" was the food which the scavenger dogs fed upon. In looking at his Jewish, religious prestige, Paul said, even as a Pharisee who kept all of the law and had triumphed greatly with achievements, he saw all of that as insignificant compared to the grace and love of God. "For Christ's sake, I have learned to count my former gains as loss." The tragedy is that sometimes we allow our achievements, or position in society to get in the way of our being a greater minister and serving more effectively for Christ. Wherever you are on the scale of life, do not see success as something merely to be enjoyed, but see your achievements as an opportunity for greater ministry to people. Forget where you are and be open to what God can call you to be. May we not lean on our strength but on the power of God.

Some Things to Remember

There are some things that we need to forget. Let's put these behind us. But there are also some things that we need to remember. Paul said, "Forgetting those things which are behind us, press toward the mark for the prize for the high calling of God." What are some of those things that we ought to try to remember?

REMEMBER YOUR PARADOXICAL NATURE

One thing we need to *remember* is the *paradoxical nature that we have*. We all have to confess that sometimes we do good and sometimes we do evil. It astounds me how much evil I often find within my own life. I have spent decades studying the scriptures, living with holy things and being a pastor of churches. When some act is done by a terrorist group, I notice the hostility, anger, and hard feelings which it brings up in me. I realize how far from being Christian I really am. I am a long way from living the kind of life that God is calling me to be. Each of us is sinful.

The Psalmist talks about sinfulness. In the passage we read today, the psalmist speaks about the man who is deliberately re-belling against God. It is the oracle of a rebel. He plots in his bed to do evil, and he is always trying to see what he can plan to carry out his evil intention. He is unconcerned about the needs of other people. This evil person has heard of God, knows him, but has deliberately broken the covenant and moved away from God and his ways. Sometimes we discuss philosophically in Sunday School classes and other places, who are those who are the furthest away from God's grace. Are they the lost heathen in Africa who have never heard any word of God? If you read the scriptures carefully, you will discern that the people who are most out of God's favor are those who have heard his love, who have been a part of the covenant, and, then have moved away from it. They have rebelled and have said that God's love is of no significance. These persons have known God's love, have heard it, and yet they turn away from it. That indeed is one of the great tragedies — to know God's love and not to live by it. Sometimes we are sinners by rebellion, and we deliberately take that avenue. Sometimes we are sinners simply because we have taken a wrong path, and we may not know at that particular moment that it is the path that leads to destruction, or difficulty. But we go that way anyway.

I recall as a young boy, and I'm sure that none of you when you were young did things like this, but we used to turn a street sign around so that it would not mark the proper street. When somebody came that way, instead of saying Lakewood Street, which was where I lived, it would say Thomas Road and people would go in the wrong direction because of that change. Now, that is a part of the mischievousness which boys would sometimes engage in. If a driver came that way and wanted to go on a certain street, he might take the wrong road because we had turned the sign that way. His mistake might not be his own fault. He might be on the wrong road and could go a long distance out of his way. But, if he never finds he is on the wrong road, then that's his fault, is it not? Each of us may get on the wrong road for a moment or two. We may travel down the street for a short time, but surely after we have gone in some direction, we can soon sense that this is not the right road. We should quickly realize that this is not the road I should travel on because this is a way that leads me to a dead end street, destruction, and sinfulness.

One of the saddest things about the Church that sometimes is passed around is that the Church is made up of those who are just the "goody-goodies" of society. All of us are sinners. None of you is a "goody-goody," I hate to tell you. You are a sinner, just as much as I am a sinner. We may be sinners saved by the grace of God, but you can't fool me or your wife or husband or parents or children that you are not a sinner. They know full well that you and I are. And so does each of us deep down inside. The Church does not say that we have no sin, but we are sinners who come to experience the grace and forgiveness of God. We reach over to invite others who are sinners to come in to share and experience the great forgiving grace of God which leads to the abundant life. We need to remember that in the beginning of this new year, *we are still sinners*. We still *need* the forgiving grace of God. We still need opportunities to begin again and again.

REMEMBER SOME DIFFICULT TIMES

I hope also that in this New Year you and I will remember some of the *difficult times* we have experienced in the past. Don't just forget them. Remember them. If we do not remember them, then we shall never learn any lessons from them. If you and I have gone through difficult times, then don't just focus on the difficult times, but see what there was in this experience or difficulty that can enable you and me to live more creatively now. Learn from the difficulty. Learn how to be a better person because of it. The experience may teach us how to act better toward others. We should learn how to avoid the same kind of problems or similar problems in the future. A minister friend of mine who lost his wife said that, through that dark, deep tragedy, one of the great lessons that he has learned is that he will never go to the home of a grieving person again without a deeper sense of compassion and understanding. He really knows what grief is now. As we remember our difficulties from the past, hopefully, they will enable us to be better persons because of the lessons we have learned from them. Remember them and learn from them.

REMEMBER THE AVAILABLE STRENGTH

Thirdly, remember also the *available strength* which each of us has. We do not face difficulties, burdens, or problems alone. Paul tells us in this passage about the power and presence of God which is available to us as we move toward the high calling of God. The Psalmist tells us about the refuge which is found in the shadow of the wings of God. He speaks about the wings that undergird us and uphold us. Remember the available strength that comes to you from God in times of temptations, or when life is filled with burdens and problems. None of us faces them isolated or alone or in our own resources or our own strength. There is the power and presence of God to sustain us and undergird us.

A young man had given in to a temptation in his business and a friend was talking to him and asking him why he had done it. And he said, "You will just never understand the external pressures that were put on me." And his friend turned to him and asked, "Man, where were your inner braces?" You and I, when we face the problems and difficulties of life, need to sense the inner braces that come to us with the strength, power, and presence of God to sustain us.

REMEMBER TO BE TOLERANT

I hope also in this New Year that you and I will *remember to be more tolerant*. Paul tells us that he has not yet arrived. "I am still in route. I am pressing toward the mark." I have not yet arrived. I am like the athlete who is running to cross the finish line. I am still running, still engaged in following Christ. One of the saddest things in life is for any person, especially for a Christian, to hold himself or herself up as though he or she has some superior intellectual grasp of Christianity, and everybody else is seen as inferior. They say in essence, "I am a more mature Christian than you." This attitude makes us intolerant of others in their understanding of Christ and in their Christian pilgrimage. We use only our understanding to measure what it means to be like Christ.

Frederick Sontag wrote a book a couple of years ago entitled *The Crises of Faith*. A devastating book review was written about his book in *The Christian Century*. Dr. Sontag wrote a letter to the editor of *The Christian Century* and said in essence this: "I did not expect everybody to agree with what I said in my book. But I guess I was really dumbfounded by the vicious attack that my fellow Christian made upon me personally. He treated me as though I were not a member of the faith. Why could he not examine my book and, even if he disagreed, see that we were fellow soldiers fighting on the same side in the war?" "We regard a brother," he noted sadly, "as if he were a savage enemy and treat him accordingly because we think that his doctrine and behavior constitute a perversion of faith."

I do not understand that kind of approach for a brother or a sister in the faith either. I remember a teacher I had in school who would accept no answer except the answer he wanted. Unless you believed as he believed, your belief was not acceptable. He rejected every other approach but his approach. We need to be more tolerant of others and understand that our theological view is not the only view that one can have to understand what the essence of the

Christian faith is. In our religious knowledge, we are all infants and mere children in route seeking to become more like God. I hope we shall remember that.

REMEMBER TO PERSEVERE

Then lastly, as Paul says in our Scripture text, we have to keep on. *We are called to persevere.* Don't quit or give up. Sometimes when we remember certain things and forget other things we are not sure which way to go because the struggle is often hard.

Many of you like I did probably stayed up recently and watched several football games. As you know, some of the games went into double overtime. All of the players continued to do their very best as long as they could. Of course a team finally lost, but each team had persevered and given their best. That's all that any of us can do in life. We are called to offer our best as long as we can.

I don't know if you enjoyed reading the comic strip Calvin and Hobbes by Bill Watterson or not, but I did. Maybe you saw this one several years ago. Calvin is walking along talking to his toy tiger. "I am getting disillusioned with these new years," Calvin says. "They don't seem very new at all! Each New Year is just like the old year. Here another year has gone by and everything's still the same! There is still pollution and war and stupidity and greed! Things haven't changed! I say, 'What kind of future is this?!' I thought things were supposed to improve! I thought the future was supposed to be better!" As they walk along through the snow Hobbes observes, "The problem with the future is that it keeps turning into the present."

And our future will! So we have to learn to know how to live in the present. I hear people say all the time, "Well, I don't make any resolutions" or "I don't know how to make any." So this morning I want to help you reflect on some resolves for the New Year. The following are some things I have thought about for myself and for some other folks I know. *Think about these.*

Resolve to forget grudges, hatred, resentments, failures, achievements, hurts, misunderstandings, sins which have been forgiven, past mistakes, wrongs, criticisms, sharp words, caustic language, curses and degrading gestures. Forget those.

Resolve to remember to be kind, to encourage others; apologize when you are wrong or when it will just help. Visit the sick; be faithful in worship and in the financial support of your church. Pray and meditate more regularly, discipline your body, mind, spirit, manner, tongue, and temper. Praise others and not yourself; smile and laugh more. Find time to help, to listen, and to assist others. Telephone, email, text or write someone you have not seen in a long time. Let them know you are thinking about them. Spend some time alone, walk, meditate, sit, pray, reflect, think, be still and quiet. Get more sleep and rest, and also exercise more. Turn off the TV and talk or read a book. Relax and play more.

Be more optimistic, grateful and expressive. Correct a bad habit, set new goals, start a new hobby. Work in Sunday School, serve on a church committee, be more faithful in your church support, help in preschool, be a children or youth teacher, or help in other places where you are needed. Share the good news of Christ with a friend. Invite somebody to church. Tell your wife or husband, children or parents that you love them more often; hug them more; be more understanding and caring. Resolve to love God with all of your heart, soul, mind and strength and your neighbor as yourself. Strive to seek first the kingdom of God.

You don't have any resolves that you can make for the New Year? I have suggested a few I know I can use, and I know that some of you can resolve to live differently, too.

O God of new beginnings, we thank you for this New Year and the gift it gives to us to begin again. May we spend the gift of this time wisely as we invest our life and energy in it. Through Christ, who has redeemed us in our time, we pray. Amen.

"WHAT COLOR IS LOVE?"

GENESIS 1:27
GALATIANS 3:26-29

Brooks Hays, who was at one time a congressman from Arkansas and a Southern Baptist, used to tell a story that is a favorite of mine. It is about a young preacher who went to his first church in a rural section of Kentucky. The first Sunday in his new church he stood up and preached a ringing sermon denouncing horse racing. After the service, one of the deacons took him aside and gently chastised him. "Now, Pastor, you need to realize that a lot of our folks here race horses. They enjoy horse racing." The next Sunday he decided he would preach against tobacco. Following the service, the same deacon took him aside and said: "Now, pastor, you need to understand that a lot of us raise tobacco. In fact, part of your salary comes from the money received in raising tobacco." The next Sunday he preached against alcohol. The same deacon took him aside again and said: "Pastor, a number of our church members work in distilleries. Some of your salary comes from the money they receive from those distilleries." Frustrated, the young preacher looked at the deacon and asked: "Well, if I can't denounce those things, what can I preach ag'in?" "Why don't you preach ag'in those heathern witch doctors?" he said. "There ain't one of those within a thousand miles of here!"

THE EVIL OF RACISM

There are a lot of people who want the gospel to relate to problems and difficulties that "ain't nowhere near us." We want preaching to focus on something that is way off someplace else where it is safe and never touches our lives. Because of the historic election of Barack Obama, an African- American, as the 44th president of the United States and his inauguration on January 20, 2008, and the celebration of Martin Luther King Jr. Day on the third Monday of January each year, I have felt challenged to address a very important issue that I feel we need to consider today. I remember that the Ku Klux Klan led some rallies in Forsyth County, Georgia when I was in graduate school at Emory University. When I was pastor in Louisiana, and several pastor friends of mine had crosses burned in their yards, I wondered when one would be put in my yard. In 1987 when I was pastor of St Matthews Baptist Church in Louisville, Kentucky, the Ku Klux Klan gathered in a protest meeting on the West side of Louisville and burned a picture of Martin Luther King, Jr. On the same day a thousand or more citizens, black, white, political, religious, and business leaders of our community, gathered at the courthouse steps to take a stand against racism and bigotry. I joined them as we proclaimed loudly that our city would not tolerate racism. Since then many strides against prejudice and racism have taken place but much still needs to be done to confront this problem that still persists. I feel that it is important to seek a word from God which addresses this situation today.

In 1619 the white man brought the black man in chains to our shore. By 1715 the number of blacks had risen to sixty thousand. By 1775 there were five hundred thousand. By 1830 there were two million black people. And then by 1860 the number of slaves had swelled to four and a half million in our country. In 1863 the Emancipation Proclamation brought an end to slavery. But with it came the Reconstruction, the Ku Klux Klan, Jim Crow laws, and the John Birch Society. For years black people have struggled to find their complete freedom.

Over fifty years ago, the Civil Rights Movement slowly began its move across our country. Rosa Parks sat down in the "white only" section of a bus in Montgomery, Alabama, on December 1, 1955, and all the world stood up and saw what happened because of her action. Martin Luther King, Jr., soon became the recognized leader of the Civil Rights movement in our nation. Later the Supreme Court handed down a ruling that segregation laws were unconstitutional. In 1968 Martin Luther King, Jr., was assassinated, and racial riots swept across our country. Later there was the assassination of Malcolm X and then the rise of the Black Power Movement. Black people have made some strides. Segregation has ended in many ways in our country, but again and again the ugly head of racism and bigotry asserts itself and seeks to turn the clock of progress backwards. The Church always needs to raise its voice and challenge that kind of evil.

John Howard Griffin, a white man, dyed his skin dark and traveled incognito as a black man. Later he published a book entitled *Black Like Me*. In it he recounted his experiences of living as though he were a black man. He found that the color of his skin caused him to be rejected from restaurants, excluded from restrooms and motels, and suffer many other indignities simply because he was black. He began to feel like he was treated as an animal, simply because of the color of his skin. Much progress has been made in this area, but much still needs to be confronted.

THE DEEP ROOTS OF RACISM

Prejudice is deep-seated. It has a long history in our world. The Egyptians enslaved the Israelites, and Moses stood before Pharaoh and challenged him: "Let my people go." Later when Israel became a nation, it showed great prejudice toward other nations. In fact, they declared that everybody else was a Gentile, not as worthy as they were in the sight of God. The Greeks proclaimed that they were the superior people of the human race. The Romans saw others as inferior, especially the Syrians, whom they looked upon as dogs. The Chinese erected a wall to separate all of the heathen devils from them. People on our nation's west coast often show prejudice toward Orientals. Those in the southern borders of our country often are prejudiced toward Mexicans. Many in the Southern states are still prejudiced toward blacks. Northerners are often prejudiced toward Southerners, and Southerners are prejudiced toward Northerners. Prejudice is an awful reality in our world.

Albert Schweitzer often mentioned the impression that stuck in his memory as a young child on seeing in the town's square on many occasions the statue of a black man burdened down with heavy chains. Later Schweitzer went to Africa to minister as a medical doctor to the black man. He knew that he did not put that black man in chains, but nevertheless he felt a sense of responsibility to help ease the burden placed on him by the white man.

Oh, I know this morning you can say: "Well, I have never burned a cross in anybody's yard." "I have never thrown a rock at a person of another race." "I haven't expressed hatred toward a person of another race." But that does not mean that you and I are free of prejudice. Too often we prejudge another person by his or her education, background, social status, appearance, or skin color.

THE CHURCH CONFRONTS THIS ISSUE

The Church declares boldly that God is the Creator of all persons. God created man and woman in God's image. Paul daringly asserted that we are all one in Jesus Christ. He declared that "there was neither Greek nor Roman, slave or free, Jew nor Gentile, male or female in Christ" (Galatians 3: 28). We can also confidently say that there is no black or white in Jesus Christ. In him we are all one. At the foot of the cross the ground is level. God's love reaches through the crucified Christ to all persons. Jesus reminded his disciples: "The one receiving you receives me, and the one receiving me receives the one having sent me" (Matthew 10:40). Even a cup of cold water given to someone in need is to minister in Jesus' name. When we reject our fellow man or woman, we are rejecting our Lord. The writer of 1 John reminds us: "If anyone says, 'I love God', and hates his brother, he is a liar, for he who does not love his brother whom he has seen cannot love God whom he has not seen" (1 John 4:20).

I heard a Baptist missionary to Africa give us this picture:

> I slept, I dreamed, I seemed to climb a hard, ascending track. And just behind me labored one whose face was black. I pitied him, but hour by hour he gained upon my path. He stood beside me, stood upright, and then I turned in wrath, "Go back," I cried, "What right have you to stand beside me here?" I paused, struck dumb with fear, for lo! The black man was not there But Christ stood in his place! And oh! The pain, the pain, the pain that looked from that dear face.

RACIAL BARRIERS ARE BROKEN DOWN

This morning let's acknowledge that we are all one in Jesus Christ. Our Lord clearly taught that we are one in God's sight. When you read the gospels, it is clear that Jesus Christ began to break down all the barriers which society had erected. He called Simon the Zealot to be one of his disciples and broke the political barrier. He reached out to minister to a woman who had been caught in the act of adultery and ignored the reputation barrier. His conversation with a Samaritan woman at the city well transcended the sexual barrier. His nighttime talk with the aristocrat, Nicodemus, whom he told must be born again, and his eating a meal with Zacchaeus broke the class barrier. He told a parable which praised the prayer of a publican over a Pharisee and disregarded the religious barrier. He reached out to the poor and outcast of society and broke the poverty barrier. He made a Samaritan a hero of one of his parables and challenged the racial barrier. He praised the faith of a Roman centurion and transcended national barriers. Again and again Jesus broke the barriers which had been set up to separate persons from each other.

Remember, Jesus was not crucified because he said: "Behold the lilies of the field, how beautiful they are." He was crucified because he attempted to break down these barriers. He taught that man and woman, whatever their status in life, were loved and welcomed by God. Like its Lord, the Church is challenged to go into the world with a gospel that breaks down all barriers as it calls all men and women to become the sons and daughters of God, saved by his grace. As members of the Church, you and I are to be the salt and light in the world as we reach out to all persons to lead them to redemption in Jesus Christ.

We Are All Prejudiced

What can we do as Christian people to combat the problem of racism? First, we can acknowledge that we are prejudiced. Every single one of us can acknowledge that he or she has some kind of prejudices. I have them. You have them. None of us is free of them. They are still a part of our life, heritage, sectional background, training, community mores, and regional values. Let's acknowledge our prejudices. They are, unfortunately, a part of us. Then, let's seek by God's grace to overcome them.

When I was in college, I served as a summer missionary in the Hawaiian Islands. One day, while I was talking with a group of young people, an oriental lad raised his hand and asked: "Why did American and Southern Baptists split?" Do you know why Baptists in America decided to divide? The division was not over theological, doctrinal, ecclesiastical, or even missionary issues. In 1845 we separated from the American Baptist Convention over the question of slavery. We wanted to keep our slaves and be Christian too. Our Northern Baptist brethren thought that was wrong. Only a few years before the Methodists had divided over the same issue. A few years later the Presbyterians did the same. Today the Presbyterians and Methodists have united their respective churches in the north and south. We as southern Baptists are not united. We split about twenty years ago and formed the Cooperative Baptist Fellowship as a new form of free Baptists in the South. Too often Southern Baptists have clung to their own separation and isolation. Southern Baptists came into existence originally for reasons of prejudice. That was wrong. As individuals, we are still prejudiced. We need to pray and work to overcome our personal prejudice and the barriers that continue to separate us as Baptists and from our fellow Christians.

GOD IS THE CREATOR AND REDEEMER OF ALL PERSONS

Secondly, we need to acknowledge that God is the creator and redeemer of all persons. Let us celebrate our diversity. Let us rejoice in the wide variety of gifts and heritages that are in the world. Let us remind one another that we are one family under God, and in Jesus Christ we are one in his Church. We are created in God's image. "So God created man in his own image, in the image of God he created him, male and female he created them" (Genesis 1:27). Let us love and respect all persons regardless of their race or color.

In an address before the joint session of Congress, President John F. Kennedy said: "I ask you to look into your hearts, not in search of charity, for the Negro neither wants nor needs condescension. But for the one plain, proud, and priceless quality that unites us all as Americans: A sense of justice. In this year, the Emancipation Centennial, justice requires us to ensure the blessings of liberty for all Americans and their posterity, not merely for reasons of economic efficiency, world diplomacy, and domestic tranquility, but above all because it is right!" It is right! All persons are God's children. He is creator and redeemer of all. So let us begin by acknowledging that we are prejudiced, that diversity is a part of our created world, and learn to glory in that diversity as we see the variety of gifts in all persons.

THE CHURCH'S ROLE

Thirdly, we acknowledge that the Church is called to be the transforming element in society. It should be the showcase for the world of brotherhood, justice, and righteousness. There can be no "Check Point Charlie," no Berlin Wall, and no barred doors at the church's entrance where persons are not allowed. Anyone to whom Jesus Christ extends his hand is my brother and sister.

I wish we could say that because a person has committed his or her life to Christ, he or she is free of prejudice. But we know that is not always true. Peter is a good example of this. Even after Jesus had commissioned him to preach the gospel to all nations, he was still prejudiced against the Gentiles. In a vision on the rooftop of Cornelius, Peter was made to see that he was to call nothing common or unclean which God had created. He saw the barrier of his racial prejudice crumble. Then, he was able to preach the gospel to all persons.

Back during the racial crisis of the sixties in our nation, a missionary from Nigeria wrote: "Aside from having to do more that it sometimes seems possible to accomplish, perhaps one of the hardest things is to try to answer questions concerning racial strife and rioting in America. It is extremely hard for Nigerian Christians—who have been taught that Christ loves all nations, races and colors, and that Christians should do the same—to understand how white Christians refuse to associate in worship with those of another color who are Christians or even those who are not." It is difficult to measure the harm we do our mission work and every cause of Christ because of prejudice. When we as his church do not live as Christians, we betray our Lord.

WE ARE BRIDGE BUILDERS

Fourthly, we need to be bridge builders. We are called by Jesus Christ to be his servants in building bridges to men and women. We are to tear down fences of hatred, injustice, oppression, and hostility. It has seldom been easy to be a bridge builder. We rarely recognize the great prophets as they walk among us. Today you and I can look back and talk about how great Amos, Micah, Hosea, and Jeremiah were, but the people of their day despised or misunderstood them. History will show that Dr. Martin Luther King, Jr., was one of the great prophets of our age. He worked and died to bring justice and righteousness for minority races in our country. You and I as Baptists should take pride in the fact that he was a Baptist.

The struggle for racial justice still continues. The denial of any person his or her God-given rights is an affront to God and a denial of the creation and redemption of God. In Christ there is no north or south, east or west, slave or free, male or female, black or white, Jew or Gentile, all are one. After Cain slew his brother Abel, God asked him, "Where is your brother?" Cain responded by asking: "Am I my brother's keeper?" No, Cain. You and I are not our brother's keeper, but we are our brother's brother. We are our brother's sister. We are sisters and brothers to each other in Jesus Christ.

Let all barriers be broken. We are to be bridge builders, not fence contractors. Let us lift up those who are in need and not hold them down. Let us encourage and not discourage. Let us remove the "Keep Out" signs and erect signs that say, "Welcome." What we need is less bullying and more brotherhood. We need less platitudes and more performance. We need less arguments and more action. We need less rhetoric and more righteousness. Let our walk match our talk. Let there be an end to discrimination and the beginning of a greater practice of brotherhood. Let there be an end to bigotry and a greater practice of harmony in the world. Let there be an end to provincialism and a greater practice of freedom. Let there be an end to isolationism and a greater practice of communion. I hoped and prayed that the inauguration of President Obama would usher in a new day of racial harmony and good will among all persons of all races. Unfortunately, that has not happened. This morning as we gather together in church, let us remember that we are in the church of Jesus Christ. The Church is never merely my church, your church, but *his* Church.

There is a legend that will not die from postwar Germany. During the Nazi regime in Germany, Hitler gave an infamous edict that had to be read from all church pulpits. The edict declared that no Jew was welcome in any church and had to leave. One day a Nazi officer entered a Christian church and announced that anyone who had Jewish blood on his father's side must get up and leave. Several on the main floor got up, one in a side balcony, and one from the choir loft rose and left. Then the Nazi soldier instructed those who had Jewish blood on their mother's side to leave. This time about half a dozen more left. The legend then says that the figure of Jesus Christ the Jew, who was hanging on the cross over the altar, came down and walked out of the church.

Whenever we attempt to bring bigotry, prejudice, and racism into his church, he walks out of it and goes into the world. He came to destroy such barriers not erect them.

WHAT COLOR IS LOVE?

When my children were small, I liked to read them a book by Joan Walsh Anglund entitled, *What Color Is Love?* [1]

> *An apple is red.*
> *The sun is yellow.*
> *The sky is blue.*
> *A leaf is green.*
> *A cloud is white…*
> *and a stone is brown.*
> *The world has many things…*
> *the world has many people…*
> *the world has many colors…*
> *and each of them is different.*
> *In a garden*
> *all the flowers are different colors,*
> *but they live happily together…*
> *side by side.*

---

1   Joan Walsh Anglund, What Color Is Love? (New York: Harcourt, Brace & World, Inc., 1966).

In a forest
all the birds are different colors,
but they live happily together…
side by side.
In a meadow
all the animals are different colors,
but they live happily together…
side by side.
In our world
all the people are different colors,
and, sometimes, they live happily together
side by side.
Colors are important
because they make our world beautiful,
but they are not as important
as how we feel…
or what we think…
or what we do.
Colors are "outside" things
and feelings are "inside" things.
Color is something we see with our eyes,
but love is something we see with our heart.
An apple is red,
the sun is yellow,
the sky is blue,
a cloud is white…
and the earth is brown.
And, if I asked you,
could you tell me…
What color is love?

Let love be color-blind, as we work together, play together, serve together, and worship together. So help us God.

O Father/Mother God, we acknowledge that we are prej-
udiced. Convert us in this area as Peter was converted from his

prejudice against Gentiles on the roof of Cornelius. O Lord, touch us again and again so that we may have eyes to see your love transcending all barriers, persons, and races. Teach us, Lord, to love as you have loved, regardless of color. Through Christ we pray. Amen.

"Sacrificial Love"

Genesis 2:21-24
Ephesians 5:21-33

A number of years ago in Germany some engineers were challenged to see if they could invent a machine that most nearly imitated perpetual motion. The machine which ran the longest would be declared the winner. Many entered their machines in hope of winning. One night a man was walking through the exhibit hall and noticed that all of the machines had stopped running but one. This man, of course, had been declared the winner since his machine was still running. He asked the winner. "What does your machine do?" "What does it do?" the man replied. "It keeps on going that's what it does. Isn't that enough?"

There are many today who think that it is enough for the family just to keep on going as it is now. But others are running up flags all around us to indicate that the family is in serious trouble today. Divorces continue to rise in our land. Many are living in trial marriages. They are simply living together without bothering to get married. Single parents are common today. Often both parents work today and have become absentee fathers and mothers, and many children have been left to themselves. Communal living is still popular in some places. The gay rights movement has received freedom to practice their lifestyle, and in many states same sex marriages are legal. The family is threatened by many forces in today's society, and it is in serious trouble. Children often do not follow their parent's example of what is right or wrong. Many parents themselves seem to struggle with knowing what is right and wrong today. Mobility in our society has fragmented families and tossed them from one side of the country to the other. What response do we take to the massive problems which seem to exist in families today? Do we simply say? "Let them keep on going as they are?" But they don't seem to be going with any real direction. They are just going. Can that be enough?

THE APOSTLE PAUL'S INSTRUCTION ON LOVE IN MARRIAGE

The Apostle Paul was no stranger to the problems of family life. In our Scripture lesson for today, he wrote about married life and the significance of the love between husband and wife. Later in this same chapter, he wrote about parents and children as well. A part of our difficulty in reading this passage is that we get hung up on that section where it states that wives are to be subject to their husbands and we can't get beyond that thought to sense the real message which Paul is trying to communicate in this passage.

Think for a moment what married life was like in Paul's day. The Jewish people believed in marriage, but every day a man would get up and express a prayer of thanksgiving that he was not a Gentile, a slave, or a woman. Women were considered a part of a man's property along with all the other things which he might own. A man could divorce a woman with a prescribed number of pronouncements, but she could not divorce him. He had the right of divorce.

In the Greek world it was even worse. Promiscuity was everywhere. A man married a woman primarily to bear his legal children. He always talked about finding pleasure someplace else rather than with his wife. For the first five hundred years in the Roman Empire, divorce was unknown. But in the time that Paul was writing this epistle, divorce was rampant within the empire. Paul wrote this letter to people who were part of the Jewish community, the Greek community, and the Roman Empire. To this diverse group he wanted to communicate an authentic message about Christian family life and marriage. He wanted to strengthen their family ties and make them stronger in the faith.

THE SACRIFICIAL NATURE OF LOVE IN MARRIAGE

I want us to look at this section of Paul's Ephesians letter and see if we can draw some central themes from this passage to strengthen the family. We will focus only on three of these. The first theme which I would mention is Paul's emphasis on *the sacrificial nature of marriage*. Christ, through his sacrificial love, built a continuous· bond with his church, and Paul draws on this image to depict a relationship of sacrifice which is essential to authentic family life. A marriage cannot really be genuine or worthwhile if a person thinks that he or she always gets his or her way. In any loving relationship a price has to be paid to maintain that love. The price will have to be paid in time, effort, and energy. The other member in the marriage has the right to express his or her thoughts and give input into the relationship if there is to be any sense of togetherness.

MARRIAGE IS COSTLY

It costs us time to understand someone else and to know their feelings and needs. It costs time to learn how to find elbow room and the essential space to live with each other. Many people are unwilling to take the time and effort which it costs. Learning to live together within marriage requires a couple to share in the price which it takes to make a marriage work. A husband, for example, would like very much to have some new golf clubs, or maybe he has been thinking about buying some new fishing equipment. At the same time, his wife has been considering buying a new dress or a new coat. She knows that their children need clothes. But while they are thinking about these things, the water heater breaks down or the dishwasher goes on the blink and leaks on the floor and destroys the tile. The tile has got to be replaced and the ceiling must be fixed. Now what do they do? Does the husband go ahead and get his golf clubs no matter what? Does the wife buy her dress anyway? Or do they learn to make some sacrifices and do what is in the best interest of the family? There is a cost in working together as a family.

THE IMPORTANCE OF COMMUNICATION

One of the hardest kinds· of sacrifices which couples have to learn to make is in the area of communication. We have to pay the price to understand each other. Often we are unwilling to do that. In counseling with couples, it has been found again and again that the biggest problem between husband and wife is their inability to communicate. They simply cannot talk with each other.

A husband came home from work one day and flopped down in his chair, picked up the newspaper and began to read it. His wife could look at him and tell that something was wrong. The signals were apparent. She asked: "Honey, what's wrong?" "Nothing," he said. "I'm just tired." He ate his meal in silence that night. Then he went back into the living room and buried his head in the paper again. She knew him too well, and in a few minutes, she came in and said: "Something's wrong. Tell me what the problem is." "Well, at work today," he said, "the boss came in and told us that they were closing down the division in Louisville and that we would either have to move to California or I would not have a job at all. I'm forty-six years old, and we have two kids in college, and I don't know what I'm going to do. Which way do I turn?" They then, began to talk about their problem, his feelings and her feelings, and what to do and where to go. They communicated with each other.

Another husband came home from work, and his wife could tell that he was very irritated. He walked in, slammed the door, kicked the cat, flopped down in his chair, grabbed the paper and rattled it. With a negative note in her voice, she inquired: "What's wrong with you tonight?" He snapped back at her about how dirty everything looked at home and that she never cleaned up anything. It wasn't long before they were really into it. An argument pursued about what he or she didn't like. She didn't know that he was on the verge of loosing his job. Deep down within him, there was the fear of being without a job and not knowing which way to turn. One couple communicated with each other; the other couple just argued back and forth, and no communication took place. In a healthy marriage, it costs us time, effort and energy to be willing to talk with each other.

THE IMPORTANCE OF TRUST

Let me suggest a couple of simple rules to enable us to communicate more effectively with each other. Number one. *You can't really communicate if you don't trust each other.* In marriage through the years, hopefully, we can build up trust for each other. That trust is based on the love which we have for each other. We have learned that we can share our inner self with each other and that we will still love each other and care for one another.

NOT ALWAYS RIGHT

Secondly, *be willing to acknowledge that you are not right* all the time. None of us is always right. Be willing to admit that somebody else can have some insight which may be better than what you or I could offer as guidance.

LISTEN WITH AN OPEN MIND

Thirdly, *be willing to listen with an open mind and ears and a closed mouth.* There are times when we need to listen to what the other person is telling us and absorb it so we can reflect on it.

READ THE SIGNALS

Fourthly, *learn to pick up the signals* which one parent, wife, husband, child may send to each other when they need help or want to communicate. These signals may be telegraphed through silence, an argumentative spirit, through sighing, or crying or in other ways. Learn to be alert to the signals which one or the other person may send to the other.

CRITICIZE GENTLY

Fifth, *learn to criticize with gentleness*. Direct your criticism in such a way that you communicate to your marriage partner that you wish the very best for him or her. Marriage is not an attempt to try and get a one-up-man-ship on each other. Criticism is not the way to show that one is superior, or that he or she has more insight and more knowledge than the other.

PRACTICE TIMING

Sixth, *learn timing*. One of the most important factors in communication is to pick the right moment for conversation. There are obviously bad moments for discussing certain things with one's wife. When she is caring for the children, or they have pushed her to the point of exploding, that is not the right moment to talk about certain problems. Pick the right time with your husband or wife or your children and learn to communicate with each other no matter what the difficulty is.

COMMUNICATE WITH LOVE AND HOPE

And lastly, strive always to *deal with each other in love and in hope*. We want to communicate to our marriage partner our best desire for them in whatever happens. Jesus Christ loved his Church and laid down his life for it. Paul reminds us that our attitude toward our wife, husband or children, or parents should convey to them that we are willing to sacrifice time, energy and whatever is necessary that we might build better relationships.

THE SANCTITY OF MARRIED LIFE

The second theme which we can draw from Paul's statement is the sanctity of married life. One of the images which Paul draws upon is a comparison of Christ's love for the Church and his cleansing and consecrating it with the purifying love a husband and wife are to have toward each other. Paul compares the sacredness and holiness of marriage with the love of Christ for his Church. This means that the love which a husband and wife have for each other is an unconditional love. God's love is unconditional toward us as he has poured out his love for us while we were sinners. As God draws us to himself, we learn to care more for others, as he does. Paul reminds us that the vows which a husband or wife made to each other are sacred and holy and that they are a commitment for life. A marriage vow is a commitment which binds us together out of our love for each other and the love which Christ has for us.

NON-CHRISTIAN WEDDINGS

One of the problems in a lot of marriages is that many of the couples who want to get married in church are not really Christians. I have often wondered why non-Christians want to get married in a church. I have always wanted to say to them, "Why don't you take your paganism straight?" When a young couple gathers to be married in a church, they come into the house of God and ask God's blessings upon their marriage. Asking for God's blessing upon their marriage arises out of their previous Christian commitment to him.

OUR LOVE DRAWN FROM OUR RELATIONSHIP WITH CHRIST

Paul began this passage by stating that both husband and wife are subjected to Christ. The first word in verse twenty-one reads: "Be subject to one another out of reverence for Christ." Our commitment to each other is bound up with our relationship to Christ. The main emphasis is not that one is above the other, but that we are first committed to Christ and subject to him out of reverence.

Through his love we have experienced the power of God's grace. Marriage is sanctified by God's blessing upon it as we are subjected out of reverence to him.

UNDERSTANDING THE MEANING OF SELF-LOVE

The third theme which I will draw from this passage is one of self-love properly understood. The type of self-love that Paul was talking about in this passage is not selfishness which is our basic sin. His emphasis takes us in a different direction. Paul writes that a husband is to love his wife as he loves his own body. His wife is like a part of his own body and he a part of her. Paul then reaches back to the Genesis passage where the second Creation story is recorded. There are two Creation stories in Genesis. In the second Creation story, woman is the crown of creation. Phyllis Trible in her book *God and the Rhetoric of Sexuality* writes that the second Creation story depicts woman as the crown of creation and the fulfillment of humanity. This creation story is not intended to demean woman or to show that she is under man but to affirm that she is essential to the completion of creation. In fact, Trible is convinced that the Hebrew word for woman which comes from the phrase "this shall be called woman" does not mean subordination to man but superiority to him.[2] In this Creation story woman is taken from man's rib and God "builds" her into a woman. She is bone of his bone and flesh of his flesh. They are dependent upon each other and really subjected to each other. Just as the woman depends on the man, so the man depends on the woman. Each is essential for the other. In his creative act, God shows the closeness and dependence each has upon the other. Paul urges the Christian husband to love his wife as he loves own body. This kind of self-love directs the husband to care for his wife as he does his own body. Husband and wife have now become one flesh united in Christ.

---

2   Phyllis Trible, *God and the Rhetoric of Sexuality* (Philadelphia: Fortress Press, 1978), 101f.

LOVE IS MORE THAN SEXUAL ATTRACTION

There is far more in this passage than just a sexual theme which one might focus upon. The sexual theme is a part of the picture, and sex is an important part of marriage. Sexual appeal is often the beginning point in many relationships. A man is attracted to a woman out of a strong biological urge. A young man may meet a young woman who looks lovely to him. A young woman meets a young man and he appears attractive to her and so a relationship begins. They begin to talk and soon a courtship is underway. We need to remember that the handsome young bushy-haired, football player may have a pot-belly and be bald twenty years later. The lovely cheerleader, who was trim and in super shape in high school, may later weigh two hundred pounds. Marriage should be built on more than just physical attraction. Physical attraction is important and is always an essential part of married life.

I like the advertisement, "Run off with your wife for a weekend." Why not? Why not go off and spend some time together. I think that is a marvelous suggestion. Couples need that time of togetherness. But real love is not built just on sexual love. One of the tragedies in our society today is the emphasis that sex is the end-all of life, and the ultimate way of finding fulfillment. From this viewpoint, women are seen as bunnies and playthings which men manipulate and use for their satisfaction. Men are seen primarily as hulks and macho individuals who are utilized for sexual gratification.

One day a young teenager was talking with an older woman about marriage. This young girl said: "Oh, you will never know how much I love Jimmy. We have been going together for six months, and he is the most marvelous boy in the world." "Young lady," the older woman replied. "I want you to know that you will never know what real love is until you have been married fifty years as I have. I know what real love is."

Real love is far more than sexual satisfaction. It is living together through good times and bad times, rearing children, learning how to buy certain items, sharing with each other, sacrificing, learning the joys and tragedies of all of the fiber which makes up married life. Some of the finest lovers I have ever known have been married fifty years. They understand what the authentic nature of love is. They have learned to sacrifice for each other. They have learned to sanctify their marriages and they have learned to be loving and caring for each other during good and hard times. Paul is trying to tell us in this passage that there is a kind of healthy self-love which makes a sound marriage. We love each other as we do our own bodies.

MARITAL VOW

We make a vow to each other when we get married in church. We say we are marrying each other for better or for worse. This is an unconditional commitment that we make to the other person. A man and woman were standing before a judge one day to get a divorce. The judge asked: "Didn't you promise to love this woman for better or worse?" "Yes I did," the husband responded. "But she was much worse that I took her for." And so are we all. There is not a one of us who in some way or the other does not have all kinds of warts. As we learn to live with each other, we have to learn to care and grow in our understanding of our relationship with each other.

THE EXAMPLE OF CHRIST'S SACRIFICIAL LOVE

At the center of our understanding of marriage is the sacrificial nature of Christ's love for his church. The love of Christ for his church is our example of the sacrifices we must make for each other to sanctify our marriage. The way Christ loved his church is the pattern of how husbands and wives are to love each other. If we really do not love each other, it is difficult to like each other. As we learn to love each other more, we can learn to like each other more.

There was a young girl who had been in an orphanage for a number of years and nobody would adopt her. One day she tied a note to a rock and tossed it out the window. On the note she had written, "Whoever finds this, I love you." It was discovered by an old man. He came into the orphanage and asked to meet the one who had written the note. He met the young girl and, for a number of years, he had a grandfather-like relationship with her. They would go to the movies, for walks, and go out for meals. He needed someone to love him as well, and he extended his love to her. After he died, the young girl had to return to the orphanage. One day she sat down again and wrote a note and tied it to a rock and threw it out the window. "Whoever finds this," it read, "I love you."

THE IMPORTANCE OF TOUCH

All of us want love. We want to be able to reach out to our husband, wife, children, or parents and say to them, "I love you." One of the ways we symbolize marriage and love is through our hands. Hands can be very symbolic. Our hands can be lifted in prayer, or hands can be used to throw a grenade. Hands can be used to lift people up or to push them down. Hands can be used to caress somebody or to slap them. Hands can be used to reach out in friendship, or hands can be used to give a gesture of hostility. Hands can be joined in marriage, or hands can be used in hateful means. Hands can give money to those in need, or hands can be used to rob a bank.

In just a few moments I am going to ask husbands and wives and children, if you are near your parents, to reach over and take your husband, wife, child or parents by their hand and join together with me in prayer. Let this be a time that you recommit your life to Christ and each other and promise to try to sanctity your marriage and with God's help make it better. Would you do that?

Join hands as we pray together,

> *Sanctifying God, we know that our homes are not always what they should be or could be, but we thank you for your love and the love we have for each other. This day we pledge our love more deeply to each other and to you. Thank you for loving us even when we are not always loveable. Help us to make our homes more Christ-like. May we learn to care for each other more and to follow*

your example of sacrificial love. May we love even as we have been loved by Christ. Amen.

"THE CROWD'S REACTION TO JESUS"

PSALM 1
MARK 11:1-10
LUKE 4:16-22; 29-30

During most of his ministry Jesus was surrounded by crowds. Crowds reached out to touch him that they might be healed. Crowds hung on his words hoping to understand something more about God. Crowds were amazed at his miracles. Their voices cried out to him for help. Crowds gathered around Christ, followed him, listened to him, and hoped that somehow this one who amazed them so much might be the Messiah. In the last week of Christ's life, crowds played a very prominent part. Let's look at their reaction to Christ.

THE CROWDS WERE INSPIRED BY JESUS

During the Passover Feast in Jerusalem, the people from all over Israel came to celebrate this national feast. The Jewish historian, Josephus, estimated that almost three million people crowded the city during this time. As Jesus entered Jerusalem, the crowds were inspired by him. He came into Jerusalem riding upon a donkey. Crowds threw down palm branches and their outer garments in his pathway. They shouted, "Hosanna to the one who comes in the name of the Lord." Through this prophetic picture or dramatic parable, Jesus attempted to teach the crowd a lesson about who he was. In ancient times a king, when he was going to war, would ride into battle on a horse.

When a king rode upon a donkey, it was a symbol of peace. In the day of Christ a donkey was not looked upon as a contemptible or amusing animal. It was symbolic of peace. "He that cometh" was a phrase depicting the Messiah. Jesus drew upon the ancient picture from Zechariah and other prophets which depicted the coming of the Messiah upon a lowly beast (Zechariah 9:9). At his coming the crowd shouted: "Hosanna." Too often we think that their hosanna meant praise to Jesus. But literally the word, "hosanna" meant "save now." "Save us now," they cried. "Here comes the king, the Messiah. Save us now." The crowds were inspired by his presence and hoped that he might be the Messiah. But not all of this admiration turned to adoration. Later it would change to something else.

INCITED BY JESUS

Sometimes the crowds were incited by Jesus. In just a few short days, after the cleansing of the Temple and the arrest of Jesus, the crowds, who had been inspired to shout, "Save us now," began to scream, "Crucify him, crucify him." How quickly their attitude changed and they turned away from him. If you read the Scripture carefully, you will note that Jesus had received negative reactions from crowds before. Do you remember the response to the first sermon which Jesus preached in his hometown? They had expected a positive word from their hometown boy who had become famous. But his sermon shocked them, and they sought to stone him to death as they drove him out of the synagogue. The crowds in his own hometown turned against him.

On another occasion when Jesus had cast out the demons in the demoniac in the country of the Gerasenes, crowds tried to drive Jesus out of their country because they were afraid of him. After one of his miracles, the crowds wanted to make Jesus a king. The crowd had not always responded positively to Christ all along. Here the crowds are incited, "stirred up" according to the Scriptures by the chief priests.

Among the crowd were the followers of Barabbas. Can you imagine their reaction when they heard that there could possibly be a choice between Jesus and Barabbas? At this word all of the Barabbas supporters—the nationalists, who wanted to see the overthrow of the Roman government—packed into the courtyard. "Which one will you choose?" You can hear the crowd already shouting: "Give us Barabbas." I suspect that most of the people in this crowd were not the same people who were along the roadway shouting "Save us now," as Jesus rode by. This crowd thought that the end which they wanted to accomplish would come about by force–not law. Their goal would be realized by violence, not by love, through war—not peace. "Give us Barabbas," they cried. He symbolized for them the overthrow of the Roman government and the establishment again of the Jewish nation as a mighty military and political power. "Jesus doesn't represent that at all," they yelled "Away with him." The popularity of Jesus was also beginning to wane, even with the common people, because they began to see that he was not the kind of Messiah that they had hoped for. His message gave another emphasis. He was different.

It is often easy, isn't it, for someone to incite the crowd and turn them in a certain direction? All you have to do is view films about Adolph Hitler to see how he was able to incite crowds in one of the most intelligent nations of the world and quickly turn those people away from justice, goodness, and the Christian perspective of life to a totally different way. He was able to enforce a law which required that the cross be removed in Christian churches and replaced by a swastika. Most of the churches obeyed this injunction. "There is no god," Hitler declared, "but Germany."

Crowds can be incited to do evil. Do you remember some of the awful things crowds did during the racial turmoil in this country? You could see the anger in faces of persons filled with prejudice as black children and black adults were beaten, stoned, and driven out of towns. Remember the snarling German shepherd dogs and the fire hoses that were used against blacks in Alabama several years ago when they were demonstrating against unjust laws? Study the faces of persons you see in a mob on television. Jim Jones incited a crowd and drew disciples around him.

Later he convinced them to drink Kool-Aid which had been poisoned as a way of committing suicide. Powerful leaders can incite crowds, but they do not always achieve good ends. Isn't it strange that a person will often do something as a part of the crowd, the bunch, the gang, that he or she would never do alone? Sometimes individuals lose their sense of personal responsibility in a crowd. It disappears and a mob mentality takes over. Sometimes the crowd was stirred up against Jesus. They were incited by his presence.

RESPONDED OUT OF IGNORANCE

At other times, the crowd responded to Jesus out of ignorance. We sometimes sing the Negro spiritual, "Sweet little Jesus boy, we didn't know who you was." "Jesus," the crowd yelled, "if we had known you were the Messiah, we would have come running. Do you think we would have ever crucified him if we had really known he was the Messiah?" Of course not! Jesus looked at Jerusalem and wept, saying: "Oh Jerusalem, Jerusalem, killing the prophets and stoning those who are sent to you! How often would I have gathered your children together as a hen gathers her brood under her wings, and you would not!" (Luke 13:34). Then from the cross he cried, "Father, forgive them for they know not what they do." "For had they known it," Paul wrote, "they would not have crucified the Lord of glory."

How often, out of the ignorance, people do not respond to Christ, or turn against his way, or, hurt his Kingdom, or reject his cause. They would not do it deliberately. It is done out of ignorance. They do not know better. It is sad. Out of ignorance many turned away from Christ. Jesus was first deserted by his hometown. Soon he is deserted by his friends; then his relatives turn against him, then the crowd, and finally his eleven disciples flee. They really didn't know who he was. If they had known for certain he was the Messiah, of course, they would have responded to him in a much more positive way. It is tragic, isn't it, that ignorance sometimes feeds on prejudice, propaganda, gossip, half-truths, envy, and jealousy? The force of evil moves through the world carried forward by the stream of ignorance which touches too many shores of life. Too often we walk through life in ignorance not knowing what to do or how we should respond to many situations.

Ernest Campbell, the former minister at Riverside Church in New York City, tells a delightful story about a man who became very aggravated with his wife's affection for her cat. My telling this story does not mean I dislike cats. After all, we had a cat that lived for eighteen years. Back to the story...Every time the man came home his wife's cat was in his favorite chair. The cat would rub against him and leave cat hairs on his clothes. Everywhere he looked there was some reminder for him of that cat. His wife devoted every waking minute of her affection to that cat. Finally, he had come to the end of his rope. He put the cat in a sack with some rocks in it and pitched him in the river. When he came home from work that afternoon, he found his wife grief stricken.

"I don't know what has happened to my cat," she cried. "I simply cannot find him."

"Honey," her husband said, "I'll tell you what I will do. I will go to the office and put a notice on the bulletin board, and I'll advertise in the paper that I will pay a five hundred dollar reward for anybody who can find your cat."

"Oh that's wonderful," she said.

As he was putting that note on the bulletin board at work, one of the men commented: "Five hundred dollars! That's an awful lot of money for a cat."

"But when you know what you know," the husband observed, "you can afford to take chances."

You and I are supposed to know something. We are supposed to have a unique perspective on what God has done in the world. God has revealed himself in Jesus Christ, and the way of ignorance is no longer our way. We have seen what God is like in Christ. "I am the way, truth and the life," he declared. "No one comes to the Father but by Me." In Christ we have found a new and different way. Let our response not be out of ignorance but from the insight and wisdom of a higher way.

INTOLERANT TO JESUS

But the crowd sometimes reacted to Jesus with intolerance. The chief priest stirred up the crowd because the Scribes and Pharisees were frightened by his teachings. They already had their understanding of the law of God. They didn't want this person stirring up the crowd. They saw him as a radical. He was public enemy number one to them. Jesus was a disturber of the status quo. They had become intolerant and wouldn't allow any changes in their traditions. They had become bigots.

Bigot is a derivative of the word, "by God." "By God," they thought. "We have all of the correct insights about God." They had God behind their own fences. They understood his law. He had spoken, they had it written down, and they were the chief interpreters of his way and will. They understood his message. They told others how they were supposed to respond to it. In their mind Jesus was stirring up the crowd. "It has been said to you." Jesus declared, "But now I say unto you." "He is breaking the Sabbath laws, breaking our traditions, and breaking our laws," they asserted. "Who does he think he is?" They understood God. They were the chief interpreters of him to the world. Jesus was a heretic to them.

Doesn't it sound familiar? Within our own Baptist denomination there have been voices that cried. "God has spoken in the inerrant Bible. We, our group, are the only persons who can interpret God correctly. Look to us for infallible guidance." This group states that the pastor is the one who is supposed to tell lay persons what to believe and how to understand the Bible. The inerrantists claim that they alone have the correct understanding about God and God's way. Here is intolerance and bigotry at its worst. This kind of attitude reaches back to the first century. It's that kind of leadership which stirred up the crowd which crucified Jesus. The chief priests stirred up the crowd and incited them for their own ends and purpose. Persons who hold to this perspective are not willing to be open to God, to let him come into their life and teach them new truths or new insight or lead them into new paths for ministry. Remember every Christian is a priest before God. No one has a special handle on truth about God. God continuously works to guide us into deeper truth. When the crowd is intolerant, it is far from God.

The Indifference of the Crowd

I guess, however, most of the time the crowd is just indifferent. The crowd was made up of good folks. They were ordinary people like you and me. They were kind, loveable, but busy. They were engaged in other activities. They had come to Jerusalem to see the sights. They were on tours. They had come to visit relatives and friends. They had come to see the Temple. They had come to see all the sights of the big city of Jerusalem. They were just busy with other things. Other things had crowded out their concern for Jesus. They were indifferent.

Often the crowd is indifferent. We see evil, suffering, pain, and sin. We see needs, but too often we are indifferent to them. As someone has said, "This is the age of the shrug." Thirty-eight people stood by and watched a man drown at one of our seacoast towns. Thirty-eight people! When one started to move forward to save him, someone stopped him, "Don't get involved," they said. A crowd in a New Jersey city stood by and watched a woman beaten to death, and nobody moved to do anything. "Don't get involved." This is the age of the shrug. Stand back. Be by-standers. Don't dirty your hands with somebody else's business.

Dick Gregory, the onetime noted comedian, told about an experience he had as a young teenager. He sold newspapers and shined shoes, and things had gone pretty well that day. He went into a cafe and got himself a good lunch. He ate a bowl of chili, a cheeseburger, a coke, and a big slice of chocolate cake. While he was eating his meal, an old wino came in and asked for twenty-six cents worth of food. After he finished the meal, the owner asked him for his twenty-six cents; the wino said: "I don't have any money." The owner took a bottle and knocked him down on the floor and began to beat him. Dick Gregory said that he jumped up and said. "Leave him alone. I'll pay the twenty-six cents." The wino looked up at him and said. "Keep your twenty-six cents. You don't have to pay, not now. I just finished paying for it." The wino got up, walked toward the door, stopped, and put his hand on Gregory's shoulder and said: "Thanks, sonny, but it's too late now. Why didn't you pay it before?"

A lot of us in life respond too late. We are indifferent to the needs around us. Read the New Testament and hear the screaming cry of condemnation which Jesus Christ directed against apathy and indifference. He condemned the man who had only one talent and buried it in the ground. His condemnation was because he did nothing. The women in the parable of the foolish virgins who had no oil are condemned because they did nothing. In the parable of Dives and Lazarus where the rich man eats his fill and the beggar, sitting at the foot of his table, gets nothing from him but the scraps off his table, the rich man is condemned to Hades because he did nothing. The Church at Laodicea is described by John as a church God will "spew out of his mouth," because it is neither hot nor cold. It did nothing. Jesus said that on the day of the last judgment some people will ask why they are condemned to outer darkness. "Lord, when did we not serve you?" "When you did not do it unto the least of these my children," he responds. When they did nothing to assist those in need, they rejected their Lord. In the parable of the Good Samaritan, the greatest condemnation is directed against the priest and Levite. They passed by on the other side and did nothing. The crowd is often indifferent to the problems and needs of the world. Too often we ignore the problems of prejudice, war, child abuse, and other massive evils that exist in the world. We often walk by on the other side and do nothing.

In Bach's magnificent piece of music, *St. Matthews Passion*, the choir raises the question at the Lord's Supper which all the disciples ask: "Lord, is it I?" The chorus responds in a ringing cry: "It is I! It is I!" We as his disciples are guilty. You and I are the indifferent crowd when we walk through the problems of life without hearing or seeing them. The needs of humanity cry out for us to do something and, instead of responding to those needs, we remain disconnected, disinterested, uninvolved, and apathetic. The voice of Christ is raised in judgment against us, because we have done nothing when he has called us to do something.

THE CROWD TRUSTED JESUS

But you know what the crowd can do? There is always the possibility that the crowd can entrust. We can commit our lives to Christ and follow him. We can see in this One the way that gives us real life, hope, and redemption. We commit our lives to him by a leap of faith. All of life involves some kind of choice. You will choose. I will choose. We can choose to go the way of ignorance and indifference, or we can choose to commit our lives to Jesus Christ and follow his way to be a part of the redemptive force which is striving to change society into the pattern of Christ. We can entrust our lives to him.

Everybody has some kind of god in life. For some, their god has become alcohol. For others, it has become drugs, wealth, power, security, prestige, control, fame or something else. Turn away from that false god and let Christ be Lord of your life. Open your life to him so that everything you do in life—your play, your job, your home life—everything is guided by the spirit and power of Christ. Entrust your life to him.

The cross of Christ lifts up its ugly head in society to remind us of the way of God. We all choose which way we will go. Many years ago Isaac Watts wrote a very moving hymn which calls us to commitment;

> When I survey the wondrous cross,
> on which the Prince of glory died,
> my richest gain I count but loss,
> and pour contempt on all my pride.
>
> Forbid it, Lord, that I should boast,
> save in the death of Christ, my God;
> all the vain things that charm me most,
> I sacrifice them to His blood.
>
> See, from His head, His hands, His feet,
> sorrow and love flow mingled down;
> did e'er such love and sorrow meet,
> or thorns compose so rich a crown?
>
> Were the whole realm of nature mine,
> that were a present far too small;
> love so amazing, so divine,
> demands my soul, my life, my all.

Loving God, grant that as a part of the crowd we shall not condemn you, reject you, nor be indifferent. We respond to such amazing love and commit our lives in trust. Through Christ, we pray. Amen.

"WHERE ARE THE TRUMPETS? THE RISEN CHRIST"

HOSEA 6:1-2
1 CORINTHIANS 15:1-22

It has always been interesting to me that, whereas Christmas seems to turn the modern world on its head with everyone making preparations months in advance in a flurry of activity, Easter does not stir much excitement in the lives of people today. Easter seems to whimper in, and most people scarcely notice its coming. If it is remembered, what images come to mind — Easter bunnies, egg hunts, new clothes, new hats, vacation time, and spring flowers? Easter comes and goes without much regard. In many places, only a handful attends special Easter services during "Holy Week," or on Maundy Thursday or Good Friday. We do not seem to realize that there would be no Christmas celebration without Easter. Easter was the first church holiday — not Christmas. Easter brought the Church into existence.

Ernest Campbell, a former minister at Riverside Church in New York City, was confronted by a woman in his congregation at the church door following the Easter service.

"Where were the trumpets?" she asked.

"Beg your pardon," he responded.

"Where were the trumpets?" she continued. "We always have trumpets on Easter morning in our service."

Where are the trumpets? Where are the resounding hallelujahs within the hearts and on the voices of Christian men and women? Where are the shouts of praise and affirmation? "He is risen!" Why are our tongues silent, our voices muted, and no song employed?

THE FEAR OF DEATH

Is it because many of us, even those in the churches, do not really believe the news of Easter? If we are honest, we have to admit that the fear of death is still our paramount fear. All studies indicate that this is still true.[3] Death is the underlying fear of all persons. Many are perplexed, disturbed, confused, and uncertain about the possibility of life after death. Job's question, "If a person dies, will he live again?" is contemporary man's or woman's question. Many today feel that any belief in life after death is only a fantasy, a pipe dream, or wishful thinking. Our materialistic scientific world does not seem to make a belief in life after death plausible or possible.

Many years ago Ernest Poole wrote a novel entitled *The Harbor*. One of the characters in the story was an impatient and determined reformer, who looked with disdain on history. "History," he once observed, "is just news from a graveyard." Ah! That is the Christian affirmation at Easter, is it not? History is news from a graveyard. The graveyard where they buried Jesus Christ was not the end, because he is risen!

---

3   Ernest Becker, *The Denial of Death* (New York: The Free Press, 1973), 11ff.

The strange word: Resurrection

Resurrection is a word which still leaves us uncomfortable today, even after hearing it for two thousand years within the Christian community. The word resurrection, however, was just as strange to the Corinthians to whom Paul wrote centuries ago. The Stoics believed that a person needed to be brave and accept death as the natural end of life. The Epicureans believed that life should be enjoyed to the fullest now, because there was nothing beyond this life. Some Greeks believed that there was a spark in the soul that lived on, but that spark was not the real essence of personality. It was not the real person who survived. Paul challenged these beliefs with his startling message: "If you do not believe in the resurrection of Christ, you need to realize that the whole Christian faith tumbles!" To Paul, the resurrection of Christ was the foundation of the Christian faith.

The Early Christian Tradition

Paul began with a ringing declaration. "I am not giving you Corinthians something which is just my words. This message is not original with me; I am telling you what you have already received." Received from where? Paul's teaching was a part of the early Christian tradition which taught that Christ was crucified, died, was raised from the dead, and continues to live. At the time of Paul's writing to the Corinthian Church, they could not pick up their New Testament and read the gospel accounts of Jesus' death and resurrection. The Gospels did not yet exist. Paul's Corinthian letter, written somewhere between 50 and 60 A.D., with its references to the appearances of the risen Christ, was the earliest written testimony to the resurrection. Remember that Jesus was crucified around 30 A.D. The Gospels of Mark, Matthew, Luke, and Acts were written sometime between 60 to 75 A.D. John's gospel, which was written much later, and the other New Testament writings were likely written from 90 to 125 A.D. Paul's letter would be the first written reference to those who had seen the risen Lord, but it was based on the oral tradition and sketchy notes which some of the disciples had probably made. Paul had not originated the tradition but handed on to them what was considered the early creed of the Church – Christ crucified, dead, buried and risen again.

ACCORDING TO THE SCRIPTURES

Paul also noted that what he proclaimed to them was according to the Scriptures (1 Corinthians 15:4). The early Church believed that Jesus was raised on the third day according to the Scriptures. On the road to Emmaus, the risen Christ reminded two of his disciples, "Thus it is written, that the Christ should suffer and on the third day rise from the dead" (Luke 24:46).

Although it is difficult for us to know exactly which Scriptures the early Church saw as predictions that Jesus would rise again, several could have been in their minds. In the Suffering Servant passage in Isaiah 53:1-12, the writer foretells the triumph of the Messiah. Various psalms are quoted in the New Testament to show the fulfillment of prophecy, such as Psalm 2:1, quoted in Acts 4:25-26; Psalm 16:8-11, quoted in Acts 2:25-28; Psalm 110:1, quoted in Acts 2:34-35; and Psalm 118:22, quoted in Acts 4:11. Another likely passage from the prophets is Hosea 6:2. "After two days he will revive us; on the third day he will raise us up, that we may live before him." As the new Israel, Christ fulfills the destiny of the nations. Jesus drew on the image from Jonah 1:17 when he declared: "For as Jonah was three days and three nights in the belly of the whale, so will the Son of Man be three days and three nights in the heart of the earth" (Matthew 12:40). Although the disciples heard these kinds of references from Jesus, they did not understand their meaning until after the resurrection.

DEATH, BURIAL AND RESURRECTION

Paul then summed up the content of the Gospel in three, short affirmations: "Jesus died, was buried, and was raised on the third day." He was dead. There was no question in their mind about that. He had been flogged by Roman soldiers, nailed to a cross, and a spear had been thrust into his side to make certain he was dead. The soldiers verified that he was dead before they took him down from that cross. He was then buried in the borrowed tomb of Joseph of Arimathea. He was wrapped in a mummy-like fashion, a napkin covered his face, and his body overlaid with one hundred and fifty pounds of spices. Then the heavy, flat stone, shaped like a large wheel on a ox cart, was rolled into the track in front of the tomb entrance. It was then sealed shut and Roman guards stood watch outside the entrance to the sealed tomb. Jesus was indeed dead and buried.

THEORIES TO DENY THE RESURRECTION

Various theories have been set forth to deny the reality of the resurrection of Jesus. Several are listed below.

THE DISCIPLES STOLE JESUS' BODY

The earliest theory to try to disprove the resurrection of Jesus was proposed by the Jewish chief priests, who claimed that the disciples of Jesus had stolen his body (Matthew 28:11-13). This fraud theory was restated recently in the novel, *The Passover Plot*, by Hugh Schonfield. Imagine! The disciples of Jesus stole his body and then were willing to die for a lie! That seems too incredible to be convincing. The disciples, who had been shattered by despair and defeat when Jesus died, were suddenly transformed and given new courage when they stole his body. If the disciples stole his body and later buried it, why did they not come back and reverence his grave and make it a sacred place? The disciples were not rallied by a lie. That is nonsense!

JESUS SWOONED ON THE CROSS

Others have conjectured that Jesus merely swooned on the cross and did not really die. This theory claims that Jesus fell into a coma at the end of the sixth hour and was revived later after he was taken down from the cross and placed in his tomb. The Gospels state emphatically that Jesus died. He was flogged, nailed to the cross, a spear ripped into his side, and he was buried. Dead! Buried! He did not swoon. He was dead!

THE WOMEN WENT TO THE WRONG TOMB

Still others have suggested that the women, who came to anoint Jesus' body on Easter morning, came to the wrong tomb. As the women approached the garden, they were busy talking and in their confusion, went to the wrong tomb and found it empty. When the angel told them, "He is not here. Come, see the place where they laid him," the women became afraid and fled (Matthew 28:5-8). Having been told that Jesus was buried in the tomb of Joseph of Arimathea and Roman soldiers were guarding it, how could the women go to the wrong place? Did Peter and John also go to the wrong tomb? Whose grave clothing was found in an empty tomb? The soldiers and the priests both claimed that the stone had been rolled away from the grave where Jesus had been buried.

THE DISCIPLES HALLUCINATED

Another attempt to disprove the resurrection has been the theory that the emotional strain of the death of Jesus and the disciples strong desire to believe that he would live again caused them to hallucinate. It is hard to conceive of five hundred people hallucinating at one time. Maybe one person! Is it possible for the twelve or crowds of people to hallucinate? We have to remember that the disciples were not looking for nor did they really believe that Jesus would rise from the dead. If any of these theories are accepted, the Christian religion would be founded on a delusion.

THE RESURRECTION APPEARANCES OF JESUS

Paul claims that the church is not a memorial society but is built on the resurrection of Christ. The resurrection is the solid foundation of the Christian Church. Listen to Paul's declaration concerning the appearance of the risen Christ. In his Corinthian letter he lists six resurrection appearances of Christ. There are only ten or eleven recorded in the Gospels, Acts, and Paul's letters. Paul affirms that he first appeared to Peter, then to the twelve, to more than five hundred persons at one time, James, to all the apostles with Thomas present, and finally he appeared to him.

The gospels state that Jesus first appeared to three women, among them Mary (Mark 16:9; Matthew 28:1-10; John 20:11-18). Why didn't Paul include women on his list? Ah, women did not count for much as witnesses in that day. Paul did not want people to think that the Church's faith was based on the idle tales of women! He wanted to use what he thought would be the strongest appeal possible. People might discount the experiences of women. Yet the gospel writers record that women were the first to see the risen Lord.

The second recorded appearance of Christ occurred on Easter afternoon as two disciples of Jesus were on their way to Emmaus (Mark 16:12-13; Luke 24:13-35). He appeared also to the disciples by the Sea of Tiberius (John 21:7-14), on a mountain in Galilee (Matthew 28:16-20), and on Mt. Olivet just before his ascension (Luke 24:50). Were the last two appearances Paul's references to Jesus' appearing to more than five hundred at once? In the Book of Acts, Luke states that Jesus "presented himself alive after his passion by many proofs, appearing to them during forty days, and speaking of the kingdom of God" (Acts 1:3). Peter in one of his sermons stated that Jesus was crucified and killed "But God raised him up, having loosed the pangs of death, because it was not possible for him to be held by it" (Acts 2:24).

WHY DID JESUS NOT APPEAR TO HIS ENEMIES?

Some have asked why Jesus did not appear to his enemies. Now that is what you and I would have done, is it not? If we were in charge, we would have Jesus come back before the High Priest and say to him: "Do you want to try again?" Or "You thought you had me, didn't you?" Or we would want to slip up behind Caiaphas, the high priest, and say: "Boo! Guess who?" We would shock or frighten our enemies into believing. Jesus never attempted to convince people to follow him out of terror or by trying to dazzle them. Remember that Jesus warned his disciples that "If they do not hear Moses and the prophets, neither will they be convinced if someone should rise from the dead" (Luke 16:31).

The closest person like an enemy to whom Jesus appeared was Paul. While Paul was traveling on the road to Damascus to persecute Christians and put them to death, Christ appeared to him. Evidently there was already fertile soil in the mind of Paul regarding Jesus, because, when Jesus confronted him in a blinding light on the Damascus Road, Paul's life was forever changed.

THE MANNER OF JESUS' RESURRECTION

How did Jesus rise from the dead? The how of it is not revealed in the New Testament. We are told only that God raised him up. When Peter and John went into Jesus' tomb, they did not find that the spices weighing down the body had been hastily dislodged as if somebody had tried to remove the body quickly (John 19:39). His grave clothes were still on the tomb slab. The words in Greek describe the grave clothes of Jesus as if the body inside them had evaporated or undergone a metamorphosis. The napkin that had been over Jesus' face was left rolled up on the stone slab. The shape of the grave clothes was a convincing sign of the resurrection of Christ to Peter and John (John 20:2-10). Some kind of transformation had taken place. His physical body had become a spiritual body.

Many questions fill our mind about the resurrection. What happened to the body of Jesus? Where did Jesus get the clothes he was wearing later since his grave clothes or wrappings were left in the tomb? I do not know! What kind of body was it? We do not know! Nevertheless, it was a body. Following the resurrection, there were appearances of Jesus where he ate and drank with his disciples, (Luke 24:36-43), and was seen walking on the shore by the Sea of Tiberius (John 21:1-14). He also made his presence known by appearing behind locked doors, disappearing from their sight, and appearing in different places across many miles (John

26:19-29; Luke 24:28-50). How was this possible? I do not know! The New Testament does not attempt to answer these questions.

Leslie Weatherhead has suggested an interesting simile which might help explain what happened to the body of Jesus. He discussed his thoughts with a professor of physics at an English university. He suggested that we imagine that we are holding a lump of wax in our hand. On a cold day the wax will be hard. If you heat the wax enough, it will become a liquid. If you heat it even more, it will become a gas. By heating the wax, one increases the speed of the molecules which compose the wax. Whether the wax is a solid, liquid, or gas is determined by the speed of the molecules. Weatherhead suggested that it is conceivable that Christ may have acted upon his body in such a way "as to alter the molecular speed and make the body take gaseous form in an unusually short time."[4]

Is it not possible that God could take the molecules of his Son's body and transform them in a manner which we cannot begin to perceive? However it was done, the New Testament clearly affirms that the body of Christ was transformed and raised. The Gospels declared that his birth was a miracle, and the resurrection was also a miracle. The resurrection is the grand miracle on which our religion is based. It completed the miracle of the Incarnation — God's unique entrance into the world through Jesus Christ.

OUR PREACHING WOULD BE IN VAIN

Paul argues that if the resurrection of Christ is denied, our whole basis for believing is undercut. Notice, first, he says, if you do not believe that Christ has been raised, our preaching is in vain. Paul and the other Christians had been preaching that Christ was raised from the grave and that persons could find redemption and eternal life through a living Lord. The resurrection of Christ was the foundation on which they had based their preaching. The resurrection had been the transforming factor in the faith of the early disciples. They were eyewitnesses of the resurrection. They

---

4   Leslie D. Weatherhead, *The Manner of the Resurrection* (New York: Abingdon Press, 1959), 51-52.

believed it out of their personal experiences with the risen Lord. His death and resurrection filled their preaching. If Christ were not risen, their preaching was based on a lie, and they had no right to preach such a delusion. But Christ has been raised from the dead, Paul exclaims, and our preaching bears testimony to that reality.

Our Faith Is In Vain

Continuing his argument, Paul declares that if Christ has not been raised, then your faith is in vain. If you do not believe Jesus has been raised from the grave, your faith is empty, futile, and hopeless. Instead of standing on a rock, you are positioned on quicksand. There is no solid foundation. Without the resurrection, everything in our belief tumbles. If Christ were not raised, all of the teachings of the Church about his self-sacrifice and life given for us are a farce. Jesus himself had consistently foretold that he would be rejected, put to death, and rise on the third day (Mark 8:31, 9:31; Matthew 16:21, 20:19; Luke 9:22; 11:29). He even used the story of Jonah being in the belly of a whale three days and nights as a sign of his resurrection (Matthew 12:40). If the resurrection is not a fact, then Jesus himself was either lying or deluded. His sacrificial death and resurrection formed the basis for much of his teaching and actions. Christ has been raised and, therefore, our trust is assured.

We Misrepresent God

Paul went even further. "If Christ has not been raised, then we misrepresent God." In their preaching Paul and the other Christians had declared that God was like Jesus — caring, loving, suffering, redemptive, and sacrificial. The resurrection was seen as an act of God vindicating the life and ministry of Jesus. The New Testament usually states that Jesus "was raised from the dead" (Acts 4:10; 10:40; 13:37; Romans 4:24; 10:9; 1 Corinthians 6:14; Colossians 2:12). If God did not raise Jesus Christ from the grave, then the early Church misrepresented God. They have lied about

God's actions. Paul declared forcefully that Christ has been raised! Our preaching, faith, and view of God are not based on a lie.

The resurrection of Christ has enabled us to see God as we had never perceived God before, but it has also provided us with a new perspective from which we can see ourselves. We see God as loving and redemptive. We see ourselves as forgiven sinners, with a new beginning for our lives. The resurrection has affirmed that what Jesus taught us about God and ourselves is true. In the presence of the living Lord, we see ourselves differently.

Robert Raines tells about an interesting experience which a friend of his had when she received a leather case. It contained handwritten instructions from her grandmother that the case be sent to her granddaughter upon her death. As she opened the case, she discovered that it contained everything she had ever sent her grandmother: birthday greetings in the hand of a five-year-old; crayoned hearts on Valentine's Day; her first school picture, personal letters from a thirteen-year-old, and more. As she looked at herself through the eyes of her grandmother, it was an eerie and solemn occasion.

> "I suddenly realized," she said, "that in preparation for her leave-taking my grandmother had arranged to send her part of my life back to me; she was giving back to me all that she loved about me — only better because she was now part of it. As I sit now pondering these things, I realize anew how she had left me alone to give witness to what we had once shared together. I am a witness for her, for myself, for our friendship. And I know that in some inexplicable way, marked by the deepest sadness, the greatest joy, and a bundle of old letters, I have been made a new person through the gift I received from her.[5]

Easter is the time when we remember again what possibilities God has seen within us, his hopes and dreams for us, his guidance and love, concern and grace. Easter reminds us of the God who

---

5   Floyd Thatcher (editor), *The Miracle of Easter* (Waco: Word Books, 1980), 81-82.

made life good and wants us to see ourselves through his eyes as his children and created in his image. Easter calls us to remember whose we are and what we can be. Easter is a witness to the love and power of God and the assurance of the new creation we can be through Christ, our living Lord.

Still In Our Sins

If Christ has not been raised, Paul continues to argue, we are still in our sins. Paul and others had preached that the death of Christ on the cross brings redemption, ransom, and forgiveness. The death of Christ would have been futile without the resurrection. If Christ were not raised, we are still burdened with our sins. Without the resurrection, we are broken under our load of sin and suffering and end in despair. Paul cries: *Christ has been raised!*

In 1926 Ford Maddox wrote a novel entitled *A Man Can Stand Up*. The title reflected the reaction which soldiers had when the armistice was signed bringing an end to World War I. The soldiers had crouched endlessly in trenches for fear of being mowed down by machine-gun fire. Armistice Day was the time when a man felt he could now stand up without fear of being shot. If you take that same thought over into the spiritual realm, you might say that the resurrection of Christ has had such a profound effect upon men and women, who have been trapped in the trenches of sin and defeat that Christ has set them on their feet again. The power of the risen Christ enables us to stand up as forgiven men and women. We know that we are not still in our sins, because Christ is risen.

No Hope Without The Resurrection

"If Christ has not been raised," Paul continues, "then those who have died, have died hopeless, and without any possibility of life after death." If Christ has not been raised, there is no hope for any of us. Our hope in life after death is based on the assurance of his resurrection. To deny the resurrection of Christ is to make our Lord a liar, too. "In my Father's house are many rooms," Jesus promised, "if it were not so, would I have told you that I go to prepare a place for you" (John 14:2). The New Testament boldly declares that all who die in Christ will live again.

"If a man or woman dies, will he or she live again?" That is the question of all persons. In the novel, *Magnificent Obsession*, written by Lloyd Douglas, one of the characters acknowledges he is getting older and muses about life and whether or not it is the end.

> I've always shied off from the subject....But, of late, it has been much on my mind. I'm quite disturbed these days. I'm in a mental revolt against death. It's sneaking up on me, and there's nothing I can do about it. Death holds all the trump cards....It takes me a little longer to get out of bed in the morning than a month ago. It is just a bit harder to climb the stairs than it was last week. The old machine is running down. I don't want to die. I understand that when a man actually faces up to it, nature compounds some sort of an anesthesia which numbs his dread and makes it seem right enough; but that thought brings me small comfort. I have been accustomed to meeting all my emergencies with my eyes open, and I don't get much consolation out of the thought that I'm to be doped into a dull apathy — like a convict on the way to execution — as I face this last one.... I wouldn't mind so much if there was anything—after that.... Bobby, do you believe in immortality?[6]

Is there life after death? The Christian affirms that if a man or woman dies in Jesus Christ, he or she will live again. This is the great affirmation of the Christian faith — because Christ lives, we too, shall live. Death is not the end for the Christian, but a time of birthing from the physical world to the spiritual, from the mortal to the immortal, from the perishable to the imperishable. Death is swallowed up in victory (1 Corinthians 15:51-55).

RESURRECTION: THE FOUNDATION OF THE CHURCH

On Easter Sunday morning two thousand years later, we join the voices of millions of other Christians and exclaim: "Hallelujah!

---

6   Lloyd C. Douglas, *Magnificent Obsession* (Boston: Houghton Mifflin, 1957), 231.

Christ is risen!" With Paul, we affirm that the resurrection of Christ is the foundation of the Christian Church. It was the one thing — the only thing — that could have turned the defeated, despairing disciples into crusading evangelists for the gospel of Christ.

THREE WITNESSES TO THE RESURRECTION

There are three great witnesses to the resurrection of Jesus Christ. The first witness is the Christian Church itself. The resurrection was what founded the Church. If Jesus Christ had not been raised from the grave, there would never have been a Church. The Church came into existence because of the disciples' belief in the risen Lord. The New Testament is the second greatest witness. The New Testament did not create the Church. Disciples in the early church wrote the Gospels, Acts, and the rest of the New Testament to tell others about Jesus Christ, the risen Lord. The third notable witness to the reality of the resurrection is that the Jewish disciples changed their day of worship from Saturday — the Sabbath — to Sunday. As sacred a day as the Sabbath was to the Jews, only a miracle could make them change their day of worship from Saturday to Sunday. This miracle they declared was the resurrection of Jesus. If the crucifixion and death of Jesus were the end of his career and life, then neither the Church nor the New Testament would have come into existence. The resurrection made the difference!

Following the Nuremburg War Crime Trials, a witness testified that he avoided the gas chambers and survived by living for a time in a graveyard in Wilma, Poland. While he was living in the graveyard, a young woman gave birth to a boy. When the child uttered its first cry, the old man prayed: "Great God, hast thou finally sent the Messiah to us? For who else than the Messiah Himself can be born in a grave?" But a few days later, when he saw the baby sucking only the tears of his mother who could give him no milk, he knew that this hope would not be realized.[7]

---

7   Paul Tillich, *The Shaking of the Foundations* (New York: Charles Scribner's Sons, 1948), 165.

But ... the Christian message is that the Messiah did come from a graveyard. Death could not contain him. The power of God raised Christ from the grave. As Paul said, "Our faith is based on the resurrection. If Christ was not raised, then everything else we believe tumbles. But thanks be to God he is risen." Let the trumpets sound! Let our voices shout: "He is risen indeed!"

Ever-Living God, we thank you for the joy of this day, for the reality of a living Lord. Enable our hearts, minds, and spirits to rejoice in the glory of the resurrection. May the joy of the resurrection permeate our hearts and our daily living. In the strong name of the living Christ, we pray. Amen.

"A THEOLOGY OF ECOLOGY:
THIS IS MY FATHER'S WORLD"

GENESIS 1:27-31
PSALM 19:1-6
ROMANS 8:19-24

Several generations ago some strange new prophets appeared and began to predict the end of the world, at least an end to the quality of life as we know it. These new prophets were not religious leaders but men and women of a science called ecology. Ecology in the broader sense is a study of the environment. This science examines the cause and effect action of different kinds of life and their surroundings, and the utter dependency these systems have upon each other if the balance of nature is to be maintained. Ecologists are warning that there is a strong link between population, productivity, and pollution. Technology has dug deeply into the natural resources to meet the demands of an ever increasing population and humanity has been very much a prodigal with the garbage left over from its "horn of plenty."

AWAKENING CRIES

It is difficult for us to realize that our wasteful living has slowed down the heartbeat of nature itself. Nature has been for us a limitless "horn of plenty" and our abuse of nature's resources has left garbage and spoils and global warming which threaten to destroy the earth and all on it. Today we need to face the problem of ecology and determine what role the Christian should play in seeking a solution to this critical issue. Almost forty years ago the "Environmental Teach-in-Day" or "Earth Day" was held to demonstrate America's awakening from its naive slumber regarding ecology to a determined course of action to unite our best minds in an effort to solve this dilemma. We still have a long way to go to meet this problem.

Over the years our magazines, newspapers, and televisions have been flooded with articles and programs dealing with various phases of the pollution problem, especially global warming. I have a suspicion though, that most of us have a tendency either to turn off, tune out, or change channels when ecological programs are televised. After all, programs about garbage, trashy smokestacks, refuse and global warming are not very entertaining to watch. The very fact that we are tempted to tune out these programs is an indication of why the problem is so intense. Our apathy has allowed us to get into this mess and may well be the factor that keeps us from arriving at a solution.

AN ENVIRONMENTAL CRISIS

The environmental crisis is apparent on every hand. Barry Commoner, a microbiologist, admonished years ago that the price of pollution could cost humanity its existence. If we are going to face this problem we must overcome what some historians have called our "cowboy" philosophy of life. This philosophy believes that there will always be more land, grass, water and clean air over the next hill; so use what you want, an endless abundance lies before us. However, our ecologists and scientists are now warning us that this is simply not true any longer. The unspoiled wilderness no longer exists. Our rain forests are being "logged" and are rapidly disappearing. Our ozone layer is being depleted. Global warming is causing our polar ice caps to melt, and acid rain is destroying our trees. We are now being encouraged to view our planet as a spaceship which has a limited supply of materials to sustain life, and, if the system is not property cared for, our supply lines can become clogged and upset the delicate, essential life support systems.

Our super highways and new shopping centers, new housing developments, although very convenient, result in the destruction of millions of trees every year which cuts off a tremendous oxygen supply in our community. I know it costs more, but it would be more healthful if our contractors would not bulldoze all the trees, but leave as many standing as possible and plant as many new ones as expedient. The use of chemical insecticides such as DDT has already spread poisons which have affected the balance of nature on land, water, and in the air. The food we eat, water we drink, and the air we breathe have greater risks of cancer and other diseases.

Millions of cars and trucks are deposited along our highways and in the oceans every year. They have little value as scrap because of the expense to convert them into usable metal. What is to be done with this highway "eyesore" and metal waste? We need to find a better way to recycle them. You and I discard six to eight pounds of waste, such as paper, refuse, and organic foods every day.

DEALING WITH OUR WASTES

The United States now handles billions of tons of solid waste each year. The liquid waste generated by sewage plants alone discharges over thirty-six billion gallons of sewage waste a day, amounting to thirteen trillion gallons a year.[8] (My figures on some of these may be lower than they actually are today, because some

---

8   Judith S. Scherff (editor), *The Mother Earth Handbook*, (New York: Continuum, 1991), 128.

of my research was done several years ago. But things are worse, not better.) It is an expensive business to collect and dispose of refuse. New York City produces 28,000 tons per day of garbage which costs $4,200,000 a day and $1,533,000,000 per year to handle.[9] We spend almost as much money on garbage as we do the space program and yet it is not nearly enough to solve this growing problem.

Our style of living has created part of the problem for us. We want convenience and we are usually willing to pay almost any price for this convenience. The frozen dinners that you and I slip into the oven or the microwave dishes may take only a few minutes to prepare, and even fewer to eat, but generations will not dissolve that aluminum foil or plastic containers we cooked it in. The non-disposable bottles, we do not want to bother ourselves with returning, may survive for centuries unless some new methods are devised to destroy them. Every discarded pop bottle on the highway costs somebody hundreds of dollars to pick up. A survey of litter along a one mile stretch of Kansas highway several years ago revealed the following items: 770 paper cups, 730 empty cigarette packs, 590 beer cans, 130 soft-drink bottles, 120 beer bottles, 110 whiskey bottles, and 90 beer cartons. The average American family throws away 118 pounds of paper, 250 metal cans, 135 bottles and jars, 338 caps and jars, and several dollars worth of miscellaneous packing. Much of this cannot be destroyed. Most of the plastic containers, which we want because of the convenience, will not decay if they are buried, and they will release poisonous gases into the atmosphere if burned.

Someone has said that the only really convenient container is the ice cream cone. It is the one kind which is self-disposable! Our quest for convenience and ease has caused us to litter our whole society with junk, trash, and filth. Ask yourself how many times you have thrown some trash out the car window instead of waiting until you came to a trash container. Then we wonder why our landscapes are spoiled.

9   *Ibid.*, 136.

Air Pollution

As obvious as the refuse problem is, it is not our only problem area. Our smokestacks spew each year into the air 2.7 billion pounds of aerial garbage, composed of peroxyacyl nitrate, sulfur dioxide, fly ash, asbestos particulates and countless other noxious ingredients.[10] Men and women are able to live on the earth because of the thin layer of atmosphere near the earth's surface. Industry and automobiles have filled the air with enough chemical pollution that the last vestige of clean air has long since passed. In some cities like New York the atmosphere is so bad that a person on the street takes into his lungs the equivalent in toxic materials of 38 cigarettes a day.

Several years ago in Los Angeles, the air was so polluted that the children were forbidden to exercise but every other day, lest they breathe too deeply. Smog has killed millions of trees in the San Bernardino National Forest. Lung cancer has sharply increased and cases of emphysema have risen 500% since 1959. An autopsy study of 100 Los Angeles area youth aged 14 to 25, released in May 1990, showed that 27 had suffered severe lung damage and would have developed lung disease in less than twenty years. Air pollution is annually causing from $60 to $100 billion in damage to our environment. The American Lung Association projects that illness and death caused by air pollution costs Americans $40 billion a year in health care and related expenses.[11] Ecologists are warning us that we have upset the atmosphere to such an extent that the ice caps at both poles are beginning to melt, and we could be on the verge of a new "ice age."

The poison in the air costs each of us in small ways also. Every property owner spends at least hundreds of dollars a year on painting, repairs, etc. as a result of the damage done by aerial garbage. It has been estimated that if all the grit, which falls on an industrial, American city in a year's time, would fall in one day, the city would be buried under twenty-one feet of such particles.

10   Ibid., 103.
11   *Ibid.*, 117.

A cartoon appeared in one of our magazines recently and in it the husband and wife are shown having a meal on the apartment patio in a big city. The wife shouts to her husband: "Come quick and eat your soup before it gets dirty."

WATER POLLUTION

Look also at what we have done to our water. Our world today is covered by 326 million cubic miles of water. That seems like a lot of water, but 97 percent of it is not drinkable and is not fit to be used in irrigation because it is too salty. Two percent of the rest is contained in frozen ice caps, which leaves only one percent of all the water that we can use. Throughout the centuries this has been enough for humanity, but recently some of our streams and rivers have become so polluted that not even sludge worms can live in them. Millions of fish have been killed by municipal and industrial wastes in America's rivers, lakes, and streams.

The industrial waste and raw sewage which pours into our rivers and lakes are unbelievable. Scientists have projected that if New York City stopped pouring raw sewage into the Hudson River today, it would still take fifteen years to cleanse itself. The Cuyahoga River in Ohio was so polluted with volatile industrial wastes several years ago that it literally caught on fire and burned two railroad trusses. On some of our North Carolina and Virginia coasts, pollution of the ocean water close to the shore was so bad that the oysters were severely harmed and were not safe to be eaten. Some progress has been made over the last twenty years. The Federal government has spent over $40 billion to improve our sewage treatment plants. But EPA projects that another $70 to $80 billion needs to be spent to meet the sewage needs of future population growth.[12]

Several years ago in a *Moon Mullins'* comic strip feature, young Kayo asks the question: "Wot's this ecology everbody's talkin' about?" Upon learning that ecology is the study of the environment and solving the pollution problem, he says, "Funny name for

---

12   *Ibid.*, 129.

it ... How'd they get it?" Moon Mullins responds quickly, "From everybody goin' up to look at th' condition of his favorite LAKE and sayin', "ECHK!"

Well, "echk" is not enough to say or do. Harry P. Kramer, who served as Director of the Taft Sanitary Engineering Center in Cincinnati reported: "A few years ago the only water borne virus diseases were hepatitis and poliomyelitis. Today there are over one hundred." Water pollution is serious business.

THE POPULATION PROBLEM

These problems are all serious but we have the technological know-how to deal with these, if we only will. The greatest crisis of all is the population problem. The rapid increase in the population growth has resulted in the ever growing number of new houses, automobiles, highways, cities, etc. Some scientists have projected that it took mankind nearly a million years to reach the first billion by 1850. With incredible speed the second billion was reached in the 1920's. In 1975 we reached 4 billion. By 2000 the figure was 6.3 billion.[13] In 2015 the population is 7.325 billion[14] and by 2020 it is projected to be 8 billion.[15] This is the reason that some scientists are saying that the human race has only 35 to 100 years of life left on the earth. In his book, *The Population Boom*, Paul Ehrlich predicts that nothing can prevent millions of people from starving to death in the future. Ehrlich notes that presently millions of people, mostly children, starved to death in the sixties and seventies, but this will be nothing compared to what will soon take place in the world. Dr. Commoner has stated that the optimum population the earth can support is six to eight billion people, and that figure, he believed, would be reached by the year 2000, even if present population trends recede.

---

13 Susan J. Clark, *Celebrating Earth Holy Days*, (New York: Crossroads, 1992), 50.
14 http://www.worldometers.info/world-population. Last Accessed 11/12/2015.
15 http://ageconsearch.umn.edu/bitstream/16380/1/br5.pdf. Last Accessed 11/12/2015.

Sometimes it is suggested that science will solve the population problem for us by enabling us to go to other planets by the time the problem becomes acute. Well, even if science could do it, and we could travel to Venus, Mercury, Mars, the moon and the moons of Jupiter and Saturn, Ehrlich projects that it would take us less than 50 years to reach the same density of population as we have on earth. We might gain another 150 years that way. That is, of course, a mighty big if!

I personally do not think we are going to have that many people on the earth to worry about. The population explosion will be stopped in one or two ways. Either we are going to do something to control the population growth, or we are going to have the bloodiest, most horrible world war that we have ever known. We are not going to live in conditions that are crowded. The Church, both Protestant and Catholic, must come to grips with the issue of birth control and present genuine help to guide families in methods of planned parenthood and birth control.

About forty-five years ago in his 1970 State of the Union message, President Nixon stated, "The great question of the '70s is: "Shall we surrender to our surroundings or shall we make peace with nature, and begin to make preparations for the damage we have done to our air, to our land, and to our water?"

In a speech to African Environmentalists on March 31, 1998, President Clinton declared:

> Finally, we must act together to address the threat of global climate change. The overwhelming consensus of the world's scientific community is that greenhouse gases from human activity are raising the Earth's temperature at a troubling rapid rate. And unless we change course, seas will rise so high they will swallow islands and coastal areas the world over, destroying entire communities and habitats. Storms and droughts will intensify. Diseases like malaria, Africa's terrible scourge, already killing almost 3,000 children per day, will be borne by mosquitoes to higher and higher altitudes and will travel across

more and more national borders, threatening more lives on this continent than throughout the world.[16]

But today things are worse. In an article published on January 15, 2015 in the *Science* journal, Will Steffen who holds joint appointments at the Australian National University and the Stockholm Resilience Center, and along with seventeen other scientists warned that at the rate things are going the Earth in the coming decades could cease to be a "safe operating space" for human beings. They all argue that economic growth, technology, and consumption are all destabilizing the global environment.[17] The February issue of *Time* magazine also quotes from the same *Science* journal article and warns that our oceans are facing a "major extinction event" and from *Nature* that the rise of sea levels has been 25% faster than previously thought.[18] Pope Francis has joined the scientists in declaring that he believes that global warming is mostly man-made, and that he will publish an encyclical about ecology and the need to protect God's creation in June or July of 2015.[19]

A POLLUTION REVOLUTION

A mass movement has swept across America demanding that something be done to end the environmental destruction. This movement seems to have attracted more college students and adults than the S.D.S. or the Civil Rights Movement. Are we on the verge of a pollution revolution? I hope so! But not enough has yet been done.

How much will we tolerate before we demand that the balance of nature be restored and maintained? England was aware for decades that it needed to furnish underground sewers, but did not get around to meeting this problem until the polluted waters brought

16 Remarks by the President to African Environmentalists and Officials from the U.S. at the Botswana, Mokolodi Nature Preserve, Gabarone, Botswana, March 31, 1998, 4.

17 *The Richmond Times Dispatch*, January 16, 2015.

18 *Time,* (February 2, 2015), 16.

19 *The Richmond Times Dispatch*, January 16, 2015.

on the Cholera later and half the population died. The handwriting is on the wall and many Americans are demanding action.

An Ethical Issue

Does the Church have any role to play in this encounter or should it sit idly by and assume somebody else will take the initiative? Many ecologists have said that this is an ethical and moral question. Surely the Church needs to provide some guidelines for action. Let me make a few brief suggestions which, I feel, the Christian needs to consider.

Do Not Despair or Give Way to Cynicism

First, do not give way to despair and cynicism. Many scientific voices are saying, "It's no use. Nobody is going to do anything. So why try?" Others are saying, "It is simply too late to correct the unbalance within nature." Some scientists have said the end is so immediate that they have given up life insurance policies and predict that in one generation life will be over for us on the earth. Robert Louis Stevenson once wrote "I hate cynicism a great deal worse than I do the devil; unless perhaps the two were the same thing." As critical and difficult as the ecological problems may be, I do not believe the Christian can take the attitude of cynicism. What would life be like without hope? The Christian clings to hope instead of despair because he or she is convinced that God is present with us even in the valley of despair, and God is seeking to lead us, if we will allow, out of the foggy valley of despair to the light of hope on the mountain above. The Christian moves through life with the inner assurance that ultimately nothing can defeat the purposes of God.

A Theology of Ecology

Importantly, we need to form a theology of ecology. Do you remember seeing a few years back the comic strip of *Peanuts* where Lucy and Linus are looking out the window at the pouring rain?

Lucy says, "Boys, look at the rain...What if it floods the whole world?"

"It will never do that...," Linus replies, "in the ninth chapter of Genesis, God promised Noah that would never happen again, and the sign of the promise is the rainbow."

"You've taken a great load off my mind," sighs Lucy.

"Sound theology has a way of doing that," responds Linus.

The ecological problem is an ethical and theological issue. Bad theology can cripple the Church's approach to this dilemma. What can our theology be like?

CONFESS OUR SIN

First, let us begin by confessing our sin and repent. Some scientists have placed the blame for our carelessness on the Judeo-Christian tradition, and have interpreted this tradition to teach that the natural world existed for humanity to conquer. God gave us "dominion over the fish of the sea, and over the birds of the air, and over the cattle, and over all the earth." (Genesis 1:26) Paul Ehrlich has stated: "The Earth has come largely under the control of a culture which traditionally sees man's proper role as dominating nature, rather than living in harmony with it..."

The following commentary was written several years ago by a high school student from Pennsylvania.

> In the end, There was Earth, and it was with form and beauty.
> And man dwelt upon the lands of the Earth, the meadows and trees, and he said, "Let us build our dwellings in this land of beauty."
> And he built cities and covered the Earth with concrete and steel.
> And the meadows were gone.
> And man said, "It is good."
> On the second day, man looked upon the waters of the Earth.

And man said, "Let us put our wastes in the waters that
the dirt will be washed away."
And man did.
And the waters became polluted and foul in their smell.
And man said, "It is good."
On the third day, man looked upon the forests of the
Earth and saw they were beautiful.
And man said, "Let us cut the timber for our homes
and grind the wood for our use."
And man did.
And the lands became barren and the trees were gone.
And man said, "It is good."
On the fourth day, man saw that animals were in
abundance and ran in the fields and played in the sun.
And man said, "Let us cage these animals for our
amusement and kill them for our sport."
And man did.
And there were no more animals on the face of the
Earth.
And man said, "It is good."
On the fifth day, man breathed the air of the Earth.
And man said, "Let us dispose of the wastes into the air
for the winds shall blow them away."
And man did.
And the air became filled with smoke and the fumes
could not be blown away.
And man said, "It is good."
On the sixth day, man saw himself; and seeing the
many languages and tongues, he feared and hated.
And man said, "Let us build great machines and destroy
these lest they destroy us."
And man built great machines and the Earth was fired
with the rage of great wars.
And man said, "It is good."
On the seventh day man rested from his labors and

the Earth was still, for man no longer dwelt upon the
Earth.
And it was good.

The biblical concept, however, does not depict us as lord of
creation in our own right. We have no right to subdue the earth to
satisfy our own ends, but men and women are stewards, responsible
to God. The curse of pollution could be the warning sign of God's
universe flashing the alarm that men and women have abused our
environment. We have often sinned against our environment;
our prodigal behavior now threatens to upset the harmony of the
universe. As God's stewards, we must learn to abide by both the
natural as well as the moral laws of the Creator.

The parable of the prodigal son seems to reflect the problem
today between humanity, God, and nature. The son had inherited
so much from his father but took what he had and "wasted his
substance," and began to be in want. The ancient parable becomes
a mirror which reflects twentieth-century man and woman's delin-
quent attitude toward our responsibility with the natural world. We
have wasted our environment and stand on the verge of world-wide
famine and environmental disaster. We live in such an affluent
society that we are not aware that thousands of people starve to
death every day. Right now! Let me give just one example. It is
estimated that five million Indian children die from malnutrition
each year. Hunger has been called the "chief killer" of humanity.
Unless a solution is found quickly for the population crisis, massive
famines are predicted throughout much of the world. The Church
has a responsibility to encourage men and women "to come to
themselves" and seek ways to begin an agricultural revolution to
feed the hungry and find the means to challenge humanity to adopt
better means of birth control.

GOD IS CREATOR AND LORD OF CREATION

Second, acknowledge God as Creator and Lord of creation.
Men and women have forgotten that we have only a delegated

dominion over nature from God. We are lord of creation only as we act as stewards who are responsible to God. (Genesis 1:26-28; 2:7) Who owns the earth? The whole of creation belongs to God and we must learn to live in harmony with it. The story of the rebellion of Adam and Eve reflects the struggle of every person to be masters of the earth and to be free from God's control. It is man and woman's desire to be our own god. (Genesis 3:5) If we try to take over "the controls" of nature without any regard for the natural laws which God has established, we succeed only in upsetting the natural order and balance of the universe and threaten our own extinction. Humanity is commanded to "subdue the earth" only in the light of a prior claim which is to live in harmony with the God who created the natural world. "The earth is the Lord's and the fullness thereof; the world, and they that dwell therein." (Psalm 24:1). God has placed us in the world to be "caretakers" and stewards of the earth.

REVERENCE ALL OF LIFE

Third, let me challenge you to reverence all of life. The ecological problem may have forced us to heed voices that have sounded so strange in calmer times. The teaching of reverence for all life, both lower and higher forms, championed centuries ago by Francis of Assisi, has been presented sharply in the writings of Albert Schweitzer. Ponder his words: "The essence of Goodness is: Preserve life, promote life, help life to achieve its highest destiny. The essence of Evil is: Destroy life, harm life, hamper the development of life."[20] He continues his argument by stating further:

> But already the world is beginning to
> recognize that the ethics of reverence for
> life, which requires kindness toward all
> living organisms, accords with the natural
> feelings of thinking men.
> By ethical conduct toward all creatures,

---

20   Albert Schweitzer, *The Teaching of Reverence for Life*, (New York: Holt, Rinehart and Winston, 1965), 26.

we enter into a spiritual relationship with
the universe.
In the universe, the will to live is in
conflict with itself. In us, it seeks to be at
peace with itself.
In the universe, the will to live is a fact; in
us, it is a revelation.
The mind commands us to be different
from the universe. By reverence for life
we become, in profound, elemental and
vital fashion, devout.[21]

EDUCATION AND COMMITMENT

Finally, let us determine our need for education and commitment instead of despair and apathy. Let us resolve to become
involved in the revolution to combat the ecological problems. It is
easy to despair and it is easy to do nothing. We have been informed
from so many quarters about the pollution crisis and must be able
to recognize that we and our attitudes are all part of the problem.
As Pogo would say, "We have seen the enemy and he is us." Let us
begin where we are, where we live, work, and play.

We need to inform ourselves and educate our community
about the local, national, and world-wide pollution problems, especially global warming. Let us search our community and isolate
the causes of pollution here. Contact your neighbors, schools,
industries, city council, mayor, senators, governor, presidential
candidates and advise them of your concern and indicate that you
want to see action to correct the situations. You may have to write
letters, send telegrams, telephone, vote, get petitions signed, speak
before civic groups, or get TV or radio time to plead your case.
Sometimes we feel that local citizens cannot do a great deal to
alleviate the pollution problem. We can all recycle our cans, glass,
plastic bottles and containers, and newspapers. We can teach our
children the importance of recycling and select a portion of high-

21 *Ibid.*, 27.

way to clean up the litter and teach our children not to litter our highways, parks, lakes, rivers, oceans, and playgrounds. That is a small start we can all take in our own homes.

Several years ago, the *U.S. News and World Report* carried an account of more than a dozen communities, both large and small, and what they did to arouse their communities to the problems and the results that were attained. The writings of leading ecologists, such as Barry Commoner, Lamont C. Cole, René J. Dubos, Eugene P. Odum, Paul R. Ehrlich, Bill McKibben, Judith Scherff, and others may be found in your library or book store.

An aroused citizenship can also demand new and more rigid laws to control and prevent pollution and stop global warming. The Federal government has strong laws in the Federal Air and Water Quality Acts and other laws which the U.S. Environmental Protection Agency (EPA) is charged to enforce to make the air, water, and land safer. These laws need to be clearly understood, updated and enforced. Congress and industry will respond to an aroused and vocal public reaction to pollution problems. Let us not let greed from oil or other industrial companies dominate but let justice and righteousness prevail.

Sometimes we wonder if one person or one church can really make any difference in the struggle against pollution or any of the other world-wide issues. The impact of one person can be seen in the powerful story that Greg Barrett relates in his book, *The Gospel of Father Joe*. Father Joe is a non-conformist Catholic priest who has ministered for thirty-five years in Bangkok, Thailand. Over one hundred million children are without education in that part of the world. His Church of the Holy Redeemer, the Mercy Centre and AIDS hospice are located in one of the world's worst slums on the edge of poverty where persons are captives of a desperate economy. Through his church, the Mercy Centre and thirty-two preschools, he has touched the lives and taught over 70,000 children, some with AIDS. Reaching one child or parent at a time, he has voiced words of hope and encouragement to those who battle insurmountable odds. "That's how you fight terrorism, that's how you fight wars (and I could add—that's how you combat the pollution problem). With one good deed at a time, you just try to get some positive energy going."[22] So, don't despair. Let it happen.

The Christian needs to confront others with the compelling facts of what poor stewardship is doing to the environment and challenge all of us to rise up as children of God and dedicate ourselves to restoring the delicate balance of nature. As Christians we believe in hope. Barry Commoner, an ecologist prophet, declared that "We are in a period of grace. We have the time—perhaps a generation—in which to save the environment from the final effects of the violence we have done to it." And Jesus said: *"He that has ears to hear let him or her hear."* Amen.

---

22 Greg Barrett, *The Gospel of Father Joe* (San Francisco: Jossey-Bass, 2008), 267.

"SOME LESSONS I LEARNED FROM MY MOTHER"

PROVERBS 6:20-22
2 TIMOTHY 1:5-7

In the New Testament we see that Jesus often used many images from the home to describe the kingdom of God. He even spoke of our future home in heaven as a place that would have many rooms. It seems appropriate on Mother's Day for us to reflect on the home. I want to reflect on the home in a different way today. My mother died November 3, 1996, and her birthday is May 14th. Around Mother's Day I always think about my mother, not only because of Mother's Day, but it is her birthday time, too. So I would like to share with you today, "Some Lessons I Have Learned from My Mother." Maybe you can reflect, as I speak, on some lessons you have learned from your own mother.

My mother died on Saturday night, and my brother did not tell me until the next morning. I was not there and I regretted that. Emily and I were going to leave after the Sunday service to go to Lynchburg, Virginia, our home town. I knew she had been in the hospital, but she had gone there several times before. My brother had said, "Don't come, she is fine." After I learned she had died, I decided to preach that morning, though it was difficult. I mused to myself, "What would be changed if I don't preach?" We could not change anything then. I informed the congregation at the conclusion of the service that my mother had died. Many of them, as they came through the door, expressed their support and prayers during that time. Since my mother had visited my church several times, many of them knew her. One of our ladies came through the door and said to me, "Your mother was a beautiful lady." I looked up the word *beautiful* in the dictionary. This is what it says, "Beautiful is that which gives the highest degree of pleasure to the senses of the mind; delights by inspiring affection or warm adoration; any very attractive feature." I drew upon that theme for my meditation for the funeral service as I shared in that service with her pastor.

This morning I want to share with you some lessons from my mother's life that have been inspiring – attractive features – those which I still carry with me. The writer of the book of Proverbs reminds us not only to remember lessons from our father, but also hold on to lessons learned from our mother. He says, "Bind these around you." Sometimes, the Hebrews literally would place these teachings around their forehead. The writer affirms that the teachings of your mother can be a guide; a watchful guard and a comforting companion in your life. I have certainly found this to be true in my own life. Let me share some of these lessons with you.

Not Defeated by Defeat

The first lesson I would mention is this; my mother was not defeated by defeat. Her father died when he was thirty-two years old. She was only six. She and her two sisters were put in the Miller Home in Lynchburg, Virginia. Her brothers were placed with relatives on a farm. She and her sisters grew up in the Miller

Home until they graduated from high school. It was like, in many ways, picture images you have seen of orphanages in the movies or on TV. I have heard my mother tell us about some of the difficult experiences she and the other girls had in the home.

I remember my mother telling about a slight misbehavior, or a minor accident she once had. The officials in the home decided to punish her by cutting her hair. At that time, a woman's hair was a sign of beauty. My mother had very long, curly hair, and they cut it until it was very short. You can imagine how that affected a child psychologically. The home, in spite of these shortcomings, did provide many valuable and useful lessons for my mother and her sisters.

My mother came through those years in the Miller Home a stronger person. She married my father after she graduated from high school. They lived through the Depression, World War II, raising three children, the normal difficulties and ups and downs of life, and the financial struggles of living on my father's salary as a mail carrier. My mother never did give in to these difficulties. She did not fall apart. She was not defeated by hard times. She was a survivor. She did not have the help of a counselor or a psychiatrist. She did not ask the question, "Why?" but "how and what do I need to do?" She did not expect somebody else to help her; she reached back on her own resources to find the strength to meet these challenges. And she did. She came through these experiences a stronger person. She learned that it is not our position, but our disposition in life that gives us happiness.

Often, you and I may suffer failure, have some kind of misfortune, sin, or setback. Yet, you and I have to learn that one of the great messages that comes to us from God is that we do not have to be defeated by these failures. We can rise above those things that would defeat us and go on. That is one of the most powerful lessons I learned from my mother.

The Importance of Home

A second lesson I learned was the importance of the home. My mother and father were married sixty-four years. Few people have that wonderful privilege. During those sixty-four years there were three children, ten grandchildren, twenty-one great-grandchildren, and still more great-grandchildren coming along the way now. My parents were both independent persons, so I am not saying to you that our home was always ideal or perfect and never without conflict. My home was a typical home where there were different opinions. Yet, there was no question ever in my mind about the love and devotion that my parents shared for each other.

My mother believed in the importance of family meals. Our meals were always served on time. Supper was usually served at five o'clock, because my father had to go to work very early in the morning. I remember one day, (I don't know if I should share this story or not with deacons present, but I will tell it anyway), I was in a fight with a neighborhood kid around dinnertime. I had not come to dinner at the time I was supposed to be there. My mother had sent my brother, Preston, to come to get me. Preston got there and he told me supper was ready, but you know, when a kid is in a fight, he has to take on first things first. My brother stayed and watched the fight instead of going home. When we got home, not only did I get a spanking, but my brother got one as well, because he stayed and watched the fight instead of going back home. I got the spanking, not so much because I was in a fight, but because I was late for the meal.

Meals always took precedent with my mother. I was astounded recently when I heard on television the suggestion that every family ought to have at least one meal a week together. My family always had our evening meal together. Dinner at noon on Sunday was always a special time together around the table.

When my parents got older, my mother faithfully took care of my father in his declining health. Nobody could take care of dad like mom could. Dad thought that nobody could fix butter beans, corn pudding, or ham biscuits like my mother could. It did not make any difference how good somebody else cooked; the food was never prepared just like Elsie could fix it. When my father would get ready to go to bed at night, he would say, "Elsie, come unmake my bed." I do not know how many husbands expect their wives to unmake their bed for them, but my mother did it for my father up until the time he died. Now, I think there were several things going on here. One, she had the bed made up in a certain way, and she did not want him to mess it up. But he also had become very dependent upon her. Home, was to me, a place where there was love and support. The significance and importance of family life were some of the valuable lessons I learned from my mother about home.

A GOOD HOME AND A WORKING MOM

The third lesson I learned from my mother is you can be a working mom and still have a good home. My mother stayed at home with us when we were small children, but when we were in high school, she began to work outside the home. This is fifty years ago! My mother worked in a drugstore and in a bookstore. Later, she was a receptionist in a funeral home. She worked several years in a sheltered workshop with children who were handicapped and mentally impaired. She had a wonderful relationship with them, and they loved her.

Although she worked outside the home, we still had a hot evening meal and always had Sunday dinner together. My mother showed us that, although she worked outside the home, she was still a mom who gave us love, understanding, guidance, and taught us what a good home was like. Many mothers today are working. I know that it is not always easy, but our family time can still be structured to make life worthwhile. It is important to learn how to relate effectively together in our home.

THE IMPORTANCE OF HARD WORK

Another lesson I learned from my mother was the importance of hard work. Both of my parents were hard workers. We always had gardens, sometimes on both sides of our house. The lots were vacant and we would plant gardens there. My mother would can or freeze vegetables from those gardens. My mother worked in the gardens and we were told, "You pick the vegetables, do the weeding, and carry your load too." Later, as children we would sell vegetables in the neighborhood. For spending money, I cut grass in my neighborhood. I had a whole list of customers up and down several streets. At first, I would get thirty-five cents for cutting those yards with a push mower. By push mower, I mean, no motor. I would push the mower with a little bag on the back to catch the grass clippings. The most I ever got for any of those yards was seventy-five cents. Later, I delivered papers, raked leaves, and shoveled snow for neighbors. Then, in high school, I worked in a grocery store, did construction work in the summer, and other jobs to earn money. My parents expected us to work hard, as they worked hard. It was a part of life.

My mother not only grew vegetables, but she also had a beautiful, manicured yard. She raised roses that were spectacular. We also had to do our share of the work in that yard. Friday was always the day that the floors were waxed. Sometimes, as children, we were a part of the polishing crew as well. We learned the importance of hard work and that there is no disgrace in getting dirt under your fingernails from hard work. My mother taught me that no matter who you are in life, you could work with your hands.

A small boy wrote in the little book, *Children's Letters to God*, "Dear God, I am doing the best I can. Signed, Fred." My mother taught us to do the best we could with what we had, where we were. She taught us the value of hard work. I heard John Mackey, a pastoral counselor in North Carolina, say the other day that he grew up on a farm. His father always taught them, "No playing, until the chores are done." That message still resounds in my head today, "There is no play until I have finished my work." I am convinced that more of us would be better persons if we understood the value of hard work.

THE IMPORTANCE OF ORDER, DISCIPLINE AND NEATNESS

Another lesson I learned from my mother was the importance of order, discipline and neatness. I did not drop my clothes on the floor and leave them in my mother's house for her to pick up. I picked them up and put them in their place. I was taught to put my clothes in the proper place. My wife has never had to pick up towels or clothes after me. My mother taught me that the proper place for my clothes was in the closet, in the drawers, or back on the hanger. When I was a child, I learned lessons quickly or they were reinforced on the rear-end if I did act properly. Neatness and order were valuable lessons from my mother. She taught me that everything has a place and everything is in its place.

This lesson is still an important part of my own life. She impressed upon me the realization of the importance of order and neatness. A part of this philosophy was that I should seek to be as attractive and neat as I could be with what I have, and wherever I am. She stressed that I was to take care of my property, clothes, and whatever I had. These were valuable lessons.

As significant as these lessons are, my mother taught me the value of honesty and integrity. She taught me to be truthful, to seek to do those things in life that would always bring honor to the family. A familiar refrain was, "Remember who you are." Many times when I was going out someplace, I heard that reminder: "Remember who you are?" I think what she meant by that was this reminder. "You are our son. We don't expect you to do anything that is going to disgrace our name or bring dishonor to our family. Remember who you are."

SUPPORT AND LOVE

One of the interesting lessons I learned from my mother was not so much by something which was said, but which came from her support and love. When I was a small boy, I went down into the woods near our home and started a fire in the woods. Soon the fire got away from me. I tried to put it out, but, as a small child, I simply could not control it. I ran back to our house and sat in a small rocking chair in my room. I rocked back and forth. I could hear the fire engines as they came to put out the fire. My mother did not have to ask, "Who started that fire?" She knew. I was sitting in my room, rocking in my chair. She knew who had done it, because I was not down there watching. My mother did not spank me for that particular experience, but I learned a lesson from her support and love. This kind of lesson and many others were conveyed by a sense of presence, encouragement, love and support.

THE IMPORTANCE OF CHURCH

My mother started me to church when I was a child. We always went to church on time and clean. We went, because she thought it was an important place for the values, meaning, and support of life. When we went through my mother's papers after her death, we found a birthday greeting card she received from her Sunday School teacher with her picture on it as a small baby. This card was on her first birthday. Here is the greeting from her Cradle Roll superintendent,

> What shall we ask for these little eyes?
> Open them, Lord.
> To see in Thy word wondrous things.
> Light them with love,
> And shade them above with angels' wings.

My mother knew that Sunday School and church could be an important place to set eternal values for my life.

The Value of Humor

I also learned from my mother the value of humor. Yes, there is hard work, but there is also a time to laugh and play. My mother had a ringing laugh, and loved to tell and hear funny stories. My mother had a way of hearing a story and then, when she would tell it later, elaborate on it. Her stories always got bigger. You might have heard a story one time, but the next time you heard it, it got bigger. There might have been five persons the first time, next time there were ten people, and the next time there might be twenty people. She had a way of letting her story grow. We as a family could laugh in the light of all her expansion.

I have learned so often in life that we can all get along better when we learn how to laugh at certain things. We should realize that sometimes we, ourselves, are laughable. We take ourselves too seriously and cannot see our own faults. We need to delight in the Lord and see what a wonderful, marvelous, and mysterious world that we have been given as God's gift. Humor is one of God's great gifts.

Age Gracefully

I think one of the most important lessons I learned from my mother is how to age gracefully. My mother never looked her age. She always was youthful looking. She lived to be eighty-five, but you would never have thought she was eighty-five years old. She always was delighted when she was with my sister June, brother Preston, or me, and someone would say, "It's good to meet your sister." She loved for people to talk about how young she was. She was always attractive and youthful looking, even at eighty-five. She loved her children, grandchildren, great-grandchildren. She always sent us birthday cards and special remembrances, because we were important to her and she remembered us.

There was a little girl who lived next door to my mother named Laura Wooley. When she was eight years old, she wrote a little poem-letter to my mother. My mother was probably eighty-two at

that time. The poem-letter was entitled, "My Best Older Friend,"
by Laura Wooley.

> My best older friend is Mrs. Tuck.
> She is my neighbor.
> Sometimes we talk together.
> I don't know how old she is.
> I think she is fifty-two.
> We plant bulbs most of the time.
> She likes flowers.
> I love her very much.
> She loves me too.
> Sometimes I play in her basement.
> I hope she lives a long time.

My mother loved children. All of her life, as she aged, she
taught us some valuable lessons about how to live in the present,
to do the best you can, and to try to be as independent as you can
be. Yet, as she reached the point she could not be independent,
she let her children and grandchildren offer her help and support
to guide her through the difficult ways that lay ahead.

A Festive Christmas Celebration

I cannot conclude today without saying what a celebrated
and festive time my mother made of Christmas. Christmas was
always a great spectacle in our home. My mother loved to deco-
rate. Our house was always brightly decorated with lights, colors,
and ornaments. There was always a Christmas tree with glowing
lights. For many years, the tree was always a cedar tree. She would
give us many presents, sometimes more presents than I am sure we
deserved. Some of our presents were clothes. Christmas was the
time when she gave us many of our clothes for the whole year. Each
one was wrapped in colorful packages. There were always some toys
and books as well. When we were small children, we always came
down the steps on Christmas morning to the song on the record
player, *Here Comes Santa Claus.*

Even as a minister today with my understanding of the importance of knowing the sacredness of Christmas, the sense of the celebrated side, the joyful side, the festive side of Christmas is still an important part of my Christmas celebration. I learned from my mother the importance of festive times like Christmas and birthdays. We never forget these times in our family life. We celebrate them.

LIVE LIFE MEANINGFULLY

My mother taught me many things, but one of the most important lessons is learning how to live life meaningfully. Someone has said, "A good thing to remember, and a better thing to do, is to work with the construction gang, and not with the wrecking crew." Some of us go through life trying to see what we can tear down. My mother helped me to see that it is far more useful to give my life to helping build up something. This is true whether it is my own character, where I live, or where I work. I should always strive to make life better.

Washington Irving wrote these words a long time ago, but the message is still important today:

> Oh, there is an enduring tenderness in the love of a mother to a son (and a daughter) that transcends all other affections of the heart. It is neither to be chilled by selfishness, nor daunted by danger, nor weakened by worthlessness, nor stifled by ingratitude. She will sacrifice every comfort to his convenience. She will surrender every pleasure to his enjoyment; she will glory in his fame and exalt in his prosperity; and, if adversity overtake him, he will be the dearer to her by misfortune; and, if disgrace settle upon his name, she will still love and cherish him; and; if all the world beside cast him off, she will be all the world to him.

This day, I am grateful to God for my mother and the lessons that I have learned from her. I encourage you, this day, to reflect on what your mother means, or has meant, to you. And, if your mother is still alive, use this day to express your love and appreciation to her. Distance often separated me from my mother. I always called her on Sunday afternoon. I still miss that opportunity today. Let us be thankful to God for lessons from our mothers.

Oh, gracious God, we thank You for the marvelous gift of life. We thank You this day for our mothers and for what they have meant to us and for the lessons we have learned from them. Teach us to use these lessons wisely, and to seek to serve You more faithfully. Through Christ Jesus, our Lord, we pray. Amen.

"Forgetting to Remember"

Deuteronomy 4:9-10
1 Corinthians 11:23-26

Several years ago I stood in Arlington National Cemetery watching the changing of the guard at the tomb of the Unknown Soldier. I recall the feeling I had as I stood there before the grave that symbolized those who had sacrificed their lives for our country and who bore no identity. You may have seen on the news or read in the paper the account of a young soldier, who had died in Vietnam, who was interred in the tomb of the Unknown Soldier. This is another reminder to remember. This is Memorial Day weekend in our country. It means different things to different people. To some folks, it simply means that they get Monday off and don't have to work. They get a long weekend, and some use it as a time to travel. Some can remember back far enough when this day was called Decoration Day. Many used to wear a poppy or some other kind of flower decorations to stress what this day symbolized. For others, it will be a time of reflection, as they re-

member those in their own immediate families whom they lost
during times of war. It is Memorial Day weekend. It is a time for
us to remember. Too many of us do not remember very well. We
often forget to remember.

A CALL TO REMEMBER

Several years ago I also stood in two other national cemeteries,
one at Vicksburg and another at Gettysburg. These, along with the
one at Arlington, cause one to reflect, on all the people who have
died in war. Row after row of crosses stretched before me. Those
crosses symbolize someone in somebody's family who had given his
life for our country. Those crosses symbolize somebody's son, father,
husband, and in some cases they symbolize a mother, daughter, or
a wife. They represent someone who laid down his or her life for
our country. But how quickly and easily we forget those sacrifices
in times of peace and calm when there appears to be no threat of
war upon us. We have a tendency also to forget the horrors of war
and to glorify war. Too often we think that war will make things
better and set things right. But how many times has war really
succeeded in doing that?

A chaplain in the First World War tells of meeting with a group
of new recruits in what was once a French wine cellar in the darkness of night. He said some of the young men had just come over
from the states. They were fresh, young, bright-eyed, and some of
our best. Soon they were to go into the darkness of that night into
no man's land, and he knew that none of them would return. As
these young soldiers gathered together to get their instructions and
pray with the chaplain before they left, they began to sing a hymn:

> Lead kindly light amid the encircling gloom.
> Lead thou me on.
> The night is dark and I am far from home.
> Lead thou me on.

Then they went out into the darkness of that night and sacrificed their lives for freedom and their country. We forget sometimes

that our wars cost us some of the best young men and women that we have. Too quickly and easily we move back into war.

Wars We Have Experienced

We were a nation that began in war with the Revolutionary War. We fought to receive freedom because we did not want taxation without representation. But, as some wag has said: "Suppose the colonist today could see taxation with representation." Few of us realize how many taxes we pay on all the items that we buy. Taxes make up a huge chunk of everything that we buy. And think we fought a war that we might be free from a lot of taxes! The War of 1812 was waged that we might be free from the interference of foreign governments in our country's affairs. The Monroe Doctrine was established to demonstrate that we would not allow any foreign country to invade our territory and interfere with our nation's internal affairs. But, even after that war, today only ninety miles from our shores in Cuba, there is a country that for many years fed revolutionary ideas and supplies to countries around and within our own territory. Thankfully, that seems to be changing today.

The Civil War tore our nation in half. I remember that my Professor of History always wanted us to call that war the War Between the States and not the Civil War. Well, that war was won, and our union was preserved, but we still have prejudice and hatred within our own country. Sometimes one state pits itself against the federal government or against another state for its rights. The Spanish American War was one that many of us are not even sure why that war was fought. Was it not something about territory and border rights? The cry of "Remember the Alamo" calls us to remember sacrifices and those who lost their lives there. But are all our border problems solved, especially with Mexico? World War I was the war that was fought, it was said, to free the world for democracy. In spite of that war, we are told today that four countries a year are lost from the democratic way of life. World War II was fought so we might have freedom. We wanted to be free from want, to have freedom of speech, freedom from fear and freedom of religion.

Freedom of religion for some people means freedom from religion. Many died to have the freedom to worship and now many do not worship at all. We fought to have freedom from fear, and yet many people today are paralyzed with fears of all kinds both internally and in relationships with other people. We have freedom of speech, and yet what has happened to this freedom of speech today is that it has been distorted and twisted to support pornography and other kinds of lewd ventures. We entered the Korean War to save a nation that today is still divided. We engaged in the Vietnam War to save another nation, and there is still no solution in that country. We engaged in two wars in Iraq where we sought to set up a new democratic government there with questionable success.

THE ESSENTIAL LESSON

Wars have been fought for a long time. One of the great tragedies of our history lessons is that we do not learn from them the essential lessons. Instead we often become like the very people whom we have defeated. In the Old Testament, we read where Israel defeated its enemy, and then returned from battle to bring back the gods of the defeated nation. Israel then sets up these gods and bowed down before them and worshiped them. They worshiped the gods of the enemy that they had just defeated.

War is not the solution to all of the problems of the world. The Christian Church needs to be the agency in society that constantly lifts up its banner and cries against the forces of war and militarism in the world today. We need to state that there is another way, and it is the way of peace.

Some of the older folks may remember this particular poem which was published years ago:

> In Flanders Field the poppies grow,
> Beneath the crosses row on row,
> That marks our place, while in the sky
> The lark still bravely singing fly.
> We are dead. Short days ago, we lived,

> Felt dawn, saw sunset's glow, but now we
> Lie in Flanders Field.
> If you break faith with us who die,
> We shall not sleep,
> Though poppies grow in Flanders Field.

Many today do not even know where Flanders Field is. But we have broken faith with those who have died, because we have not learned why they died. We have also not learned from those deaths the necessary lessons to enable us to be better persons in the world today.

LESSONS FROM THE DEAD

In some funeral homes and pathology labs there is a statement written in Latin, *Mortui Vivos Docent*, "The dead teach the living." What lessons will we learn from the dead so that you and I shall live more effectively today? The book of Deuteronomy draws for us a significant lesson in learning from the past. In the scripture passage which we read this morning, we have a record of a portion of a sermon. The whole fourth chapter in that book contains a sermon. It was a sermon delivered to the people of Israel calling them to remember. They were reminded to remember what God had done. The preacher was calling them back to remember the first commandment; "You shall worship the Lord your God." "Lest you forget." Remember. Carve what God has done for you in freeing you from Egypt in your memory. Understand it, discuss it, interpret it, memorize it, and live by it. Remember God's covenant. Be grateful and faithful. Remember God. Teach your sons to remember, and let them teach their sons, and we would also say today, our daughters and their daughters. Let this truth pass from one generation to another so that they might be instructed in the way of God. They are reminded that they cannot live the true life when their covenant is violated with God. They are challenged to learn to live under God's covenant relationship.

REMEMBER TO BE GRATEFUL

The prophet advised them to remember so they would be grateful. They are reminded to be grateful to the God who led them for forty years while they wandered in the wilderness. It was he that preserved them. Remember the God who freed them from bondage and brought them into the Promised Land. It is a call to be faithful. Be faithful to the God who has delivered you and has given you freedom. It is a call to commitment. Commit yourself to this God who loves you and has given you freedom in this day. Remember lest you forget. So the children of Israel, down through the ages, have called their people to gather for a Passover meal and to teach their children what God had done for them. This tradition is passed on to the next generation so they, too, will remember what God has done for them.   Paul reminds us of Jesus' words at the Last Supper, "Do this in remembrance of me."   Remember!

Many of us, however, do not pass on the lessons we have learned. They are too easily and too quickly forgotten. Oh, I know we do not like to talk much about sacrifice today. We do not want to sing about "Fountains filled with blood, drawn from Immanuel's veins." That sounds like archaic theology to us today. To talk about sacrifice and commitment seems like something we modern persons do not want to be bothered with. We are part of the egotistical and selfish generation in which only number one is important. This attitude directs us to look out for ourselves. We are not concerned with other people. We are concerned with what life can do for me, my, and mine. This approach is not directed to what we can do for others to make their load lighter and easier as we go through life. But when you and I choose that way, we choose the way that is opposite to the Christ-like way. Selfishness is not the Christ-like way.

Sometimes we also falsely identify our burdens, struggles, and problems which we bear as what is meant by Christian sacrifice. I remember one summer sitting in the congregation of Ebenezer Baptist Church in Atlanta, Georgia, and hearing Martin Luther King, Sr. preach. He was retired at that time but was supplying on the Sunday my family worshiped there. I have always remembered one of the things he said in that sermon. He said a lot of folks talk about bearing crosses in life. They identify the cross that they have to bear with a sick mother, or a sick father, or a sick child, or some other kind of burden. That, he said, is not the correct meaning for understanding bearing a cross. Everybody sooner or later has to bear some burdens. A cross requires an active response and not just passive submission. A cross, he declared, is something a person takes up voluntarily for others. God's Son, Jesus Christ, took up his cross voluntarily. It was not merely imposed upon him. His cross was not reduced to his problems, difficulties, or circumstances. "I lay down my life," Jesus said, "that I may take it again. No one takes it from me, but I lay it down of my own accord." (John 10:18). He voluntarily took up that cross for us. I think that is a real insight. Real love and sacrifice are done voluntarily for others. It is not simply imposed upon us by circumstances, but it is something that we ourselves do out of a depth of conviction that it is the right thing to do. We are not pressed into it by circumstances alone.

During the Second World War, in one of the awful German concentration camps at Ravensbruck, a young nun was imprisoned there from Russia. They called her Mother Maria. The whole camp including the German soldiers had grown to love her in the two and half years that she had been there. She was spoken of as "that wonderful Russian nun." She had done so many good things to help relieve the suffering of others. One day a group of women were being lead to be gassed. As they were standing in line, one of the young women began to break down and cry hysterically. Mother Maria walked over to her and said: "Don't be frightened. Look, I will take your turn." The guards did not notice her, and she went on through the line and was gassed with the rest. When the German soldiers realized the mistake that they had made that day, it stopped the gassing for awhile. The death of that good woman stopped the gassing for a little while.[23]

---

23 Colin Morris, *Mankind My Church* (Nashville: Abingdon Press, 1971), pp 87-88.

A Call to a Higher Standard

Maybe one life sacrificed voluntarily, one life becoming involved in tough and difficult situations, one life helping others in need may stop the difficulties for awhile. One person may voluntarily lift the standard and make it better for others. Oh, that doesn't mean that we always have to give our lives. But we have to give our life. There must be the willingness to step into difficult circumstances and to face the problems so they can be made better. It is not easy to go into situations that are dirty, sinful, or debased and seek to make them better in the name of Christ.

Jesus has called us to a higher standard of living than simply what can I get from life. He has called us to the standard of love, and he has told us that the commandment from him is that we love one another. Jesus has received the love from God. Jesus passes this love on to his disciples, and the disciples passed this love on to each other. There is a chain of love that comes from God the Father to the Son, and to his children, and each to the other. It is very obvious, if we do not love one another that we have either broken the chain of Christ's love or we really have to question the depth of our understanding of the Christian faith. It was said of the early Christians, "Behold, how they loved one another." If we cannot really love one another, there is a serious question about whether or not we have made the right kind of commitment to Christ, who has sacrificed his life for us. One of the saddest commentaries often on the church today is that the world no longer speaks about how Christians love one another.

Christ, Our Model for Love

Can we be a part of the community of Christ without this love? God's spirit infiltrates our lives so that hatred, envy, and all our other problems are bathed in the freshness, vitality, newness, creativity, and spirit of the Christ who gives us new birth. We seek to be like he is. Our model for love is Christ. He tells us to love others as he has loved us, and his love was given to the point of laying down his life for us. "I no longer call you slaves," he said, "I call you friends." We are no longer simply in bondage to him. There is an intimate relationship. A relationship of friendship has been established by him for us with the Father. We love God not because we must, since we are in bondage to him, but we love because he has loved us in an intimate way. "Go now and love one another," Jesus directs us. "My commandment to you as disciples," Jesus said, "is to love one another."

War time sometimes brings great sacrifices. I'm sure you recall the story of the ship Dorchester in the Pacific Ocean that was torpedoed one dark night during the Second World War. As the young sailors were trying to get to the lifeboats to abandon ship, there were not enough life jackets to go around. The four chaplains aboard gave up their life jackets so that these young sailors could be saved. As the ship, *Dorchester*, was sinking into the ocean the chaplains, one Jewish chaplain, two Protestant, and one Catholic, linked their arms and sang a hymn together as they went down with the ship.

"Greater love hath no man," Jesus said, "than he lay down his life for another." You and I may not be called upon to lay down our life for another, but we are certainly called to live our life for another. We are not to let our selfish ends, goals, or purposes become the dominant philosophy for us. We look to Christ to guide us, direct us, and inspire us. That means that sometimes the way may be difficult. We may be misunderstood or rejected. We may encounter all kinds of problems and difficulties, but, if we attempt to follow Christ and his way of love, we know that the way is good and, therefore we continue to walk in its path.

Remember. Remember the past. Remember the past, so that we can learn from that past and live a better life today and in the future. There was an ad in a church bulletin which went like this: "The Ladies Aide Society is having a garage sale. Bring those things that are too old to keep and too good to throw away. Your husbands are welcomed also." There are some things hopefully that are too good to let go, and one of the things that ought to be is the memory of what others have done for us. A memory of this kind recalls the sacrifices that many have made for our country. We remember the sacrifices of others and what they have done for us that we might live safely at this moment in history. We draw on what others have done and continue to build for the future.

WAGING PEACE

One of the hardest lessons that we have to learn, though, is the difficulty of waging peace. It is not easy, because often society kills its peacemakers. Gandhi was one of the great leaders of peace around the world. Gandhi brought his nation, India, through non-violent leadership to a point of experiencing freedom for his people. But in 1948 Gandhi was assassinated. In our own country, Martin Luther King, Jr. attempted to bring freedom for his black people from their bondage so they might experience true freedom within our nation. But in 1968 in Memphis, Tennessee, Martin Luther King, Jr. was assassinated. In that same year, Robert Kennedy, as he was campaigning on a platform for peace, was also assassinated. In March of 1980, in El Salvador, Archbishop Oscar Romero tried to speak for peace in his country and he, too, was assassinated. Why do we kill off those who want to bring peace? The Prince of Peace himself was killed. The one who told us, "My peace I give unto you, not as the world gives, give I unto you," was killed. But join their voices we must.

I hope on this Memorial Day that we shall remember the sacrifices that others have made that we might be here in this place, at this hour. The lives of many young men and women were given for us. Others sacrificed in less costly ways. I hope we shall learn from these sacrifices and that we shall go forward and wage peace in our world. I wish I were a pacifist but I am not. I am convinced that it is probably the true Christian philosophy. This indicates how far I am from having arrived in this area. We live in a world where there is sinfulness of all kinds, and we have difficulty confronting it and knowing how to deal with it. But confront it we must. Let's wage peace.

In a very moving sermon, "The Unknown Soldier," Harry Emerson Fosdick concluded it with these lines:

> I will do the best I can to settle my account with the Unknown Soldier. I renounce war. I renounce war because of what it does to our own men. I have watched them coming gassed from the front line trenches. I have seen the long, long hospital trains filled with their mutilated bodies. I have heard the cries of the crazed and the prayers of those who wanted to die and could not, and I remember the maimed and the ruined men for whom the war is not yet over. I renounce war because of what it compels us to do to our enemies, bombing their mothers in villages, starving their children by blockades, laughing over our coffee cups about every damnable thing we have been able to do to them. I renounce war for its consequences, for the lies that it lives on and propagates, for the undying hatred it arouses, for the dictatorships it puts in the place of democracy, for the starvation that stalks after it. I renounce war and never again, directly or indirectly, will I sanction or support another! O Unknown Soldier, in penitent reparation I make you that pledge.[24]

I hope that you and I as Christians can attempt to make a pledge that we, too, will attempt to live as peacemakers in our world. Remember the scriptures that instruct us: "But I say unto you do not resist one who is evil, that if anyone strikes you on the right cheek, turn to him the other also. If anyone would sue you and take your coat, let him have your cloak as well" (Matthew 5: 39-40). "But I say unto you love your enemies and pray for those who persecute you" (Matthew 5: 44). "If possible," Paul says, "so far as it depends upon you, live peaceably with all" (Romans 12:18). The writer to the Hebrews writes: "Pursue peace with everyone, and the holiness without which no one will see the Lord" (Hebrews 12:14). And our Lord himself declares, "Blessed are the peacemakers for they shall be called the sons of God" (Matthew 5:9).

---

24 Harry Emerson Fosdick, *Riverside Sermons* (New York: Harper and Brothers, 1958), pp 351-352.

On this Memorial Day, I hope that we shall not forget to remember the sacrifices that others have made. But may we also attempt to be makers of peace in the world and follow our Lord who set the example. Let us begin where we are. Be at peace with yourself, be a peacemaker in our church, community and in all the world.

> *Oh Reconciling God, we acknowledge to you that it is not easy to live in an evil world and to be peacemakers. We hear the rattling of sabers all around us and the constant threat of war. We acknowledge the disgruntleness and conflicts which are within our own nation and within us. Teach us, O God, what it means to be peacemakers, and may we learn to love peace and to wage peace, as we follow the one who is the Prince of Peace. For it is in his strong name that we offer our prayer. Amen.*

GRADUATION DAY

"AN OPEN LETTER TO CATHERINE ON HER GRADUATION FROM HIGH SCHOOL"

Your mother usually does most of the letter writing and will probably write most of the letters to you from home, but I thought I would drop you a note to congratulate you a little early. It's hard for me to realize that it is time for you to be graduating from high school because, after all, it was only yesterday that I graduated from old E. C. Glass High School in Lynchburg, Virginia. It was really, only yesterday or so it seems. It seems like it was only yesterday that we brought a bald headed baby home from the New Orleans hospital, and we worked so hard to try to find enough hair to put on a bow ribbon so people would know that we had a girl. It seems like only yesterday that you and your brother used to come rushing to the door, and I could hear you saying: "Here he comes, here he comes." I would open the door and you would run into my arms as I came home from work. Those days ended too soon for me.

It seems only yesterday that you became a barber at the age of four and gave your brother a very special haircut. It seems only yesterday that you and your brother took a ride backwards in the car down our very steep driveway when you were very small. It was only a small dogwood tree which I had planted the day before that kept you from having a serious accident. I can still see the expression on your face when you fell out of the pine tree in our front yard and broke your arm and you exclaimed:

"I wish this was a bad dream." I remember those small, petite, beautiful dresses. I remember your first solo which you nervously sang in church. I remember your first date. I remember your efforts as you ran in track trying to stretch forward to force yourself to do a little bit more. Oh, I remember. My mind is filled with so many days, places, and events. We have albums and scrapbooks filled with pictures and memories. But other parents have similar memories of their children as they reflect on many things which they want to remember from their past at this high moment. Tevye and Golda sang something of my own feelings in *Fiddler on the Roof*:

> Is this the little girl I carried,
> Is this the little boy at play?
> I don't remember growing older,
> When did they?
> When did she get to be a beauty,
> When did he grow to be so tall?
> Wasn't it yesterday
> When they were small?

It seems like only yesterday that, indeed, you were so small. The world that we adults have prepared for you is not the kind of world I really wish that you could have. Oh, I know we have done many good things. We have advances in science. We now have computers, satellites, by-pass surgery, and even transplants. We possess all kinds of modern conveniences. But in our world there is also war, murder, disease, poverty, alcoholism, and drugs. You will find some people who will cheat you, seek to hurt you, abuse you, and misuse you. They are there in the world, and I wish we could have made it better for you. But you will also find in this world that there are people who will love you, who will care for you, who will support you, and encourage you. Find them! Rally your life around them.

Oh, there are so many things I would like to say to you today, but there is no way I can say them all, and so many of them have been said many times before. But I want to remind you of two biblical figures that maybe can give you some guidance as you take the next step in your life. Remember Joseph? Long ago there was a young man named Joseph who was a great dreamer. He dreamed dreams and had visions of how God was going to use him in the world. His own brothers despised him for his dreams and wanted to put him to death. "Let's see what now will become of his dreams," they cried. There will always be people in life who will try to see what they can do to destroy your dreams and visions. I think directions for trying to hang onto the dreams and visions come to us from the words of Jesus as recorded in the twelfth chapter of the Gospel of Mark. Jesus gives us guidance in how to live life with fullness and richness when he directs us "to love the Lord our God with all of our mind, heart, soul, and strength." I hope that you will be able to utilize that truth to enable you to live a more effective, creative, and meaningful life.

I hope that you will draw upon the vision of wholeness which Jesus taught us when he spoke about loving God with your whole mind. It's ok to think as a Christian. Use your mind. Keep on using it. Love God with all your mind. As followers of the one who said "I am the Truth," the Christian is in pursuit of truth in its wholeness and not truth which is partial or fragmentary. Don't believe those people who want to make you close your mind to truth, or who want to guide you into one area of life and see it as the whole truth. There are so many people that see their business, their approach, their discipline, or their philosophy as the only sure path to all of the truth.

Do you remember how we used to take hikes up into the mountain right behind where we lived? Do you remember the deep ravine which continued part of the way up the hill? One day while I was hiking up through the woods, I came upon a spider's web which stretched across the ravine. I picked up a stick and tapped one corner of the web. The owner of that web looked around to see if it was lunch time. He crawled slowly toward where the web had moved. Then I tapped it slightly in another part of the web, and he moved toward that spot. I touched another part and he moved again. As I walked away from that web, I realized that the spider's whole world was confined to that web. He saw his world only from there. Standing apart from his web, I really did not exist for him. Don't let people tell you the whole world is their web. There will be a lot of folks who will try to do that. Life is seen only through their perspective. To assume that one sees all of life through only one perspective is a fragmentary view. Don't let people reduce your vision to a partial view of life. Seek to experience its wholeness. Use your mind, be expansive and reach out to encompass more.

When you find that "special person," I know you are going to want to carry a picture of him, but you will not carry an x-ray picture of him. An x-ray picture is a wonderful invention for diagnostic purposes, but that picture would not show a complete picture of your beloved. An x-ray is only a partial view. Too many people want us to have just an x-ray view of life. This is life seen only from a fragmented perspective and no more. Look for the broader perspective of the totality of life.

This was driven home to me recently in a story which Ernest Campbell told about a young boy and his mother watching a golfer caught in a sand trap. The golfer hit the ball again and again, but it refused to move. After his many swings at the ball, he finally threw his club away and walked off in a huff. The small boy, witnessing this scene, explained: "Mother, it must be dead now because he has stopped beating it."

There are a lot of folks in life who will beat their point into the ground to declare that their view is the only avenue to truth. Be careful around those folks. Anyone who tells you that his or her perspective is the only correct one is dangerous. They do not have the whole perspective. No one does. Learn to have a wider view of life. Use your mind. The Christian is on a pilgrimage to understand the totality of truth.

The famous German philosopher, Hegel, expressed it this way. "To think and to think hard is a religious duty." To commit your life to Christ is not a call to surrender your mind. William James, the American philosopher, once wrote: "I like tender hearts, but I like tough minds." Learn to use your mind. Tough Christian minds are those who are able to bring about what the tender hearted often want. Do not believe those people who will tell you that the Christian faith is linked with sentimental approaches. Learn to use your mind and think hard about the great issues of life. The questions of suffering, pain, war, poverty and all the others demand that you use your mind. Learn to use your mind with all of its creativity, imagination, power, and potential. Down through the centuries there have been great thinkers who have given their minds as well as their hearts in service to God and truth. Christians like Paul, Athanasius, Augustine, Aquinas, Luther, Calvin, Wesley, Schweitzer and thousands of others, have believed that to love God with all one's mind is not separate from what it means to be a Christian. These persons were aware that to be a "believer" was not divorced from being a "thinker." A Christian is not one who will believe anything or respond to every sentimental or emotional appeal. He or she is committed to loving God with one's entire mind, and that is indeed a sacred duty. Love God with all your mind.

The challenge, however, is to love God not only with all of your mind but with all of your heart as well. To the ancient Hebrew, the heart was the symbol of life. The heart was the very focal point of what it meant to be a person. When you love God with all of your heart, you are able to see life differently because you have learned to observe not only with your mind but from the inner depths of your own being. The greatest accomplishments in the world usually come about from those who have learned to see not merely with their mind but also with their heart. Use your heart to see deeper. What some people miss, these persons have learned to see. In the presence of greatness, many shrug it off as ordinary and routine. While those who have an inner vision from the heart have seen mystery and potential, others have only felt the wind, or saw the lightning flash, or heard the thunder roar. Some see the obvious, while others see visions of new life, horseless carriages, ships moving across the ocean or airplanes going into outer space. Be a seer. See beneath the surface. Dream dreams. Be a Joseph and hang onto your dream. Do not allow others to destroy them. Keep on having visions.

The word "educate" comes from a Latin root which means "to make a plant grow." You cannot make a plant grow unless you have a vision of it in your head. You cannot build a building unless you have a vision of it. And you cannot help build your life unless you have some kind of vision of the possibility of what that life can be. That is part of loving God with all of your heart.

I recall as a young student in high school that I was not motivated much to study at all. I have to confess that I used to sit in classes and read books while my teachers were teaching other subjects because often I was simply bored with what was going on. It was not until much later that a teacher lit a spark within me and gave me a vision of what education could mean to my life. I hope somebody will motivate you, stimulate you and light sparks within your life.

As you know, recently your mother and I had the opportunity to go to Ft. Myers, Florida, and we visited the home and lab of Thomas Edison. When Edison was a young boy, he was taken to school by his father and some teachers tested him and said that he was too dense to learn. Edison had only ninety days of formal education. He was considered too dense to learn! Here is a man who is considered by many today to be one of the greatest geniuses of all times. His motivation and spark came from within and he kept on dreaming and kept on working.

Remember that there will be occasions when you will fail. But that does not mean that you are a failure. There will be some times when you make mistakes, but that does not mean that you are a mistake. There will be some times when you will sin, but that does not mean that you are worthless and no good. We all fail. We all make mistakes. We all sin. But let us learn from them and build on them. Don't use the philosophy of life which I like to call the "If only" philosophy. "Oh, if only I had done this, or if only I had done the other or if only I had not done this or that." Learn to approach life with the attitude "next time." "Next time I will do this. Next time I will do that." Learn from your mistakes, build on them, and go on. Love God with all your heart.

The word truth in Greek means "unveiling of a mystery." When we love God and pursue him as the great mystery, we are unveiling the great mystery of life and we are probing into everything around us so we can grow, learn, and be open to all truth. Be a seer. Look with your heart so you can see behind the mystery to the great God who loves you, and is always seeking to give you more of life and its richness.

Love God with all your mind, and with all of your heart. But remember that Jesus has reminded us that the greatest commandment has also called us "to love God with all our soul." The word "soul" in the Hebrew tradition was a reference to the inner person, the ego. This was a way of saying; you are to love God with the very depths of your inner being. You are to love with what constitutes the authentic you. It is who you really are. That is an inner vision of awareness.

Do you remember how many times, when you got ready to go someplace, especially on a long trip, we would say to you:" Remember who you are." I'm sure that you sometimes wondered; "What in the world does that phrase, 'Remember who you are' mean?" Well, you are going to find a lot of people in life who will try to tell you who you are. We all ask: "Well, who was I and who am

I? Who are you, anyway?" Some want to tell us today that we are only fragmented personalities. Is the biologist correct are we merely complicated animals? Is the biochemist right; are we primarily a collection of elements? Is the psychologist on target when he asserts that we are basically a bundle of impulses and glandular reactions? Is the socialist accurate when she asserts that we are products of our environment? Many see us only in fragments, as parts of something. But are we not more than merely the sum of our parts? Too many try to tell us that we have no control over who we are as a person. I don't believe that.

Remember who you are. You are our daughter. You are a person of worth and importance. You are a child of God. You are a person with high values, high standards, and high morals. Remember you are a Christian. Remember to follow the Christ-like way. Remember who you are when you go into a world filled with all kinds of people who are trying now to tell you who you are. They want you to become the playgirl or playboy of life. There are those who tell us that we are what we smoke, or what we drink, or how we indulge in "free" sex. They will tell you that the longer your cigarettes, the more you drink, and the more you participate in illicit sex, the more you are somebody important. But remember who you are. There is no such thing as free sex, free drugs, or free alcohol. Each of these carries a costly tag with it. The costly nature of illicit sex is that some bring home unwanted children and lose the sacredness of sex. Others sometimes find themselves going down costly, dead-end streets which end in nightmares of alcoholism and drug addiction.

Remember who you are when those folks try to tell you that life is basically eat, drink, and be merry. Some folks will try to sell you on specializing in pleasure or to join the revival of paganism and hedonism. Their sale is the gospel according to Playboy. Remember who you are when they tempt you to engage in illicit sex, drugs, and booze to experience the "meaningful" life. It is strange that many of the persons who sing those songs of loose living and play the tunes of sex, sand, lust, and drugs often are bored, depressed, and find no meaning or direction in life. Remember who you are. You are a child of God, a person of great worth.

Oh, I want you to have fun. I want you to enjoy life. I hope you find joy, happiness, and richness in life. But find it with friends that will last. Avoid those who just want to give you a thrill for the moment or use you to satisfy their own longings for a few tantalizing minutes. Build friendships that will endure. Find friends who will stand by you, nurture you, care for you and enrich your life. Avoid those who just want to use you, abuse, or thrill you. Remember who you are.

The ancient psalmists sounded a deep insight into the nature of persons when he asked and answered: "What is man that you (God) are mindful of him?" He responds by saying that persons are created just a little lower than God. We are more than any of our fragmented parts. There is within us the image of God. God has breathed into us the very breath of his being and infused into us life by the gift of his creativity. What an awesome thought — we have been created in the image of God. We are called, then, to the highest standards - to be like God. To love God with all of one's soul is the call to excellence. It is a reminder of our creation. To remember who you are is to recognize that you are a child of God, created in his image. But you have not arrived. You are reaching toward becoming what he has created you to be, as a full authentic person, a real human being. How often we say, "Aw, I was only human," as though that is not to be anything very worthy.

To talk about becoming human is to realize what God has created you to be as his child. It is the challenge to be a full, complete, whole person as you were created to be. Keep on growing as you love God with all of your soul. High school is not the end of your education. It is the beginning. College will not be the end; it is also another beginning. Keep on growing and developing. To love God with all your soul is to be aware that your education is never complete. Each of us is always in the process of becoming. The one person I know who is the least educated and mature is the individual who says that he or she has arrived educationally.

None of us can say, "I'm done with learning." No one ever really is! In the process of becoming, we either go forward or backward. There is no area of neutrality. We are either growing or moving forward so that our mind, heart, and being are progressing or we are regressing, moving backwards.

The pop theologian, Charles Schulz, depicts in one of his comic strips Lucy and Charlie Brown engaged in conversation about school. Lucy asks Charlie Brown, "Are you smarter this afternoon than you were this morning?"

"Yes," Charlie Brown replies, "I think I'm a little smarter."

"But are you a whole lot smarter?" she asks.

"No," he responds, "Just a little smarter."

"See?" Lucy exclaims.

"See what?" Charlie Brown asks.

Lucy then asserts, "There are serious flaws in our educational system."

Many would agree that there are serious flaws in our educational system. The biggest flaw is to think one has arrived. There are a lot of folks who want to tell you that education is complete at certain junctions like high school or college. But we are always in process of developing and expanding the inner self. The inner person is to be complete and full. Keep on growing. We never arrive. It is a lifelong process. Remain open to the fullness of life before you. You are still in the process of becoming, of being, and learning.

To love God with all your soul is to hold before yourself the awareness of what you can become. It is to learn to live with God at your elbow. It is to live with the power of God's presence breaking into your life. It is to realize that the challenge of learning is ever before you and beyond you. Whether your area of study is math, science, English literature, psychology or religion, you will not arrive. Robert Hofstadter, a Nobel Prize winner in physics, expressed it well a decade or so ago: "Many will never find the end of the trail. It is ever before you and pulling you toward the not yet realized."

Remember that to love God with all of your strength is a challenge which reaches beyond the commitment of your physical muscles and energy. It is a call to discipline and high moral values for the use to which you commit your body. The word used for "strength" is concerned with discipline, order and control. Too often young people give their bodies and minds to the lowest common denominator. They have not measured their lives against standards which have been very high. They often invest their lives in cheap and easy thrills. They have not yet measured their lives against such high standards that they are willing to assert, "I'm not for sale at any price." I hope there will be those things against which you will take a stand and declare that they are too costly. Your standards are higher than those who would pull you down low.

Let Christ become the standard by which you measure your life. Through his teachings you recognize that there are limits in your life. There are times and places, because of this, that you declare "I cannot be bought." This part of your life is not for sale. You refuse to sell your birthright for a mess of pottage like a quick thrill or the easiest way. You refuse the lesser values when you are called to measure your life by the highest values and standards of all - "to be like God." Like young Timothy you are challenged to strive by these high values.

I hope you will continue to grow spiritually and that you will work at prayer. Don't let people tell you that you are outgrowing religion and that you no longer need it. Continue to rely upon prayer. Let God walk with you and draw on the strength of his presence. Oh, I don't mean you have to wear a badge that says: "Hey look, I'm a Christian; I'm a preacher's daughter." No. Let your spiritual depth be something internal in your life where there is peace, and strength from the presence of God. Find a church at college where you can worship. It will not be like your home church. Find some place to worship; locate some other fellowship which can sustain you while you are there so you will continue to grow spiritually. This will keep you from becoming immature religiously. You have a responsibility to continue to grow and nurture your inner person. I hope you will find that place soon, and your inner life will continue to grow and develop.

I hope that you will also reach for those goals, as you seek to educate yourself, where your greatest motivation for your education will not be determined primarily by how much money you make. Oh, now I hope you can be successful financially for a whole lot of reasons. We want someday to cut the cord so you can sustain yourself. But as you go to find a job in life, don't let the determining factor be just whether or not you will make a lot of money. I want to lift up my voice with a loud cry and declare that material ends are not the only goals in life. There is more to education and life than finding ways and means to acquire wealth. Meaningful living is not realized simply by climbing up the business ladder to success. You may be challenged to find greatness by giving your life in service to some cause for which you will never get rich but you will be helpful to others. You need to capture a vision of a task which demands doing, and which may get your hands dirty, and give you little material rewards, but will enrich you within and bless the lives of those you help. Your vision may lead you to a place that nobody else may want to go. And even I may be reluctant to let you go there, but, if you have a dream, a vision from God, then you listen and respond.

There are places where a lot of money may not be made, but you will give your life to helping others, stopping wrong, overcoming poverty, combating diseases, lifting up the fallen, encouraging the depressed and weary, waging peace, and most of all raising the values and standards of those you meet. We seek to prepare people to live more than a fragmented life. Sometimes, we say, you may fulfill your life the most not by becoming wealthy, but by going into the difficult places of life. Sometimes that may lead you into the slums, backwoods, small towns, jungles, or isolated areas of the world. You go to lift higher the standards and ways of life for others. This is strength which is disciplined for service and ministry. I hope you can find that kind of place and service. Find your dream and hang on to it. Just one final word. As you go, remember that your mother and I love you. We love you more than you can ever imagine or that we can ever express. Go with that sense of love.

It will not be easy for us to let you go. We have tried to teach you the high path of life. We know that we must now let you go for your own sake. In this new freedom, you will continue to grow and mature. So, we let you go for your sake. But remember that we are always there, if you ever need us. Go, and may your life be filled with peace, joy, happiness, and love. Go with the sense of God in your life. May God enrich it and make it full. We love you.

Love always,

Dad

"THE CHALLENGE OF RELIGIOUS FREEDOM"

LEVITICUS 26:12-13
JOHN 8:31-36

I had seen the famous picture of the signing of the Declaration of Independence on numerous occasions, but it was only recently that I noticed that the sun was in the picture. One can see the sun shining through a window. It is uncertain whether the sun was rising or whether the sun was setting on that occasion, and I often wonder which it was. As I reflected on that picture, I began to wonder, even more today, is the sun of liberty setting or is it still rising? Is it coming to an end or just beginning?

LOSING OUR PERSPECTIVE ON FREEDOM

We hear sounds within our country today which indicate that many people do not understand freedom very well. In fact, there are many who want to deny freedom to others while ensuring their own freedom. Many do not understand very clearly why our country was founded originally or what its basic purpose was. We continue to suffer as a nation because of that lack of awareness. "The American flag is not," as Henlee Barnett once said, "a blindfold but a bright symbol which inspires true patriots to challenge evil at every level of government." The American flag is a symbol of our country, but it is not a blindfold to keep us from seeing what we as a church should say and do to confront evil in our society. I am a loyal American, but I am Christian first. I do not think I could ever make the statement; "My country right or wrong." The pulpit, and we as Christian citizens, should always challenge our country to lift its ethical sights higher, to be what God would have this nation be.

In 1976 we celebrated the bicentennial of our country. This was a very momentous occasion and I dare say, without fear of contradiction, that few alive today will live to see the next one hundred year celebration. There may be several very young ones who might make it because of heredity or the advancement of medicine, but I think most of us will have to acknowledge that we shall not likely see that next celebration.

In 1976 there was a man who led a parade in Bartow, Florida, who was 134 years of age. Charlie Smith, who was originally from Liberia, was recognized in 1976 by the Social Security Administration as the oldest living American citizen. In 1854, at the age of twelve, he stood on a slave auction block in New Orleans and was sold to a rancher in Texas. When he was nineteen years old, the Civil War broke out. Later, he heard Lincoln's Emancipation Proclamation. He lived through numerous wars. He saw our country go through good and bad times, and he himself endured personal enslavement and suffering. From Africa to America, from slavery to freedom, from war to peace, here was a man who lived through; many generations and who understood something about freedom better, I dare say, than any of us will ever truly understand it.

On this Sunday after the fourth of July, I want us to reflect on freedom — especially religious freedom. I am aware that there

are some voices who say that the church should not get involved
at all in this kind of celebration. But the church has always been
involved, and the church should continue to have something to
say in the affairs of government. We cannot equate church and
country. Civil religion is always dangerous. We have too much of
that heresy being proclaimed from television and other platforms
today. But there is a healthy, legitimate role which religion can play
in the celebration of any event in our country.

THE BIRTH OF FREEDOM

The first observation I would make is this: freedom really had
its birth in the Hebraic-Christian religion. Contrary to what some
historians say who try to trace our understanding of democracy
back to the free city state of Greece, I believe that freedom goes
back far beyond that. It goes back to Moses who stood before the
Pharaoh of Egypt and demanded in the name of God, "Let my
people go." It goes back to the time when the God of Israel said to
his people, "I will establish my Tabernacle among you and will not
spurn you. I will walk to and fro among you; I will become your
God and you shall become my people. I am the Lord our God who
brought you out of Egypt and let you be their slaves no longer;
I broke the bars of your yoke and enabled you to walk upright"
(Leviticus 26:12-13 NEB). Even before Moses, there was Abraham
who went out looking for a city without foundations, because it
was built on the power and presence of God himself.

THE BIBLE PROCLAIMS FREEDOM

Some of our forefathers and mothers would not let the slaves
they owned read the Bible. Do you know why? They knew very
well that reading the Bible often provoked a desire for freedom in
its readers. Black slaves were not allowed to read the Bible because
slave owners feared they would see, revealed in the Old Testament
and the New Testament, God who was constantly setting his people free. The Bible resounds with cries for freedom from the God
who would move against the oppressors of people, the God who

would stand up for the slaves, the God who would stand up for the poor, the despised, the rejected, the imprisoned, the hurting, and the down and out. Someone has said that if he were a dictator and had control of a country; the one book he would not let the people read would be the Bible. Why? The Bible constantly tells us of the God who is the liberating God — the God who is always seeking to free people.

There is an interesting difference I think between South America and North America. Why has that continent not progressed as we have? I think there are two basic reasons. Its resources and climate are as fine as ours, but a part of the difference is a totalitarian government and a totalitarian church. Wherever there is a government that controls its people and there is no real freedom, there is a radical difference in how the people live, think, and act. Whenever there is a totalitarian church which tells its people what they must think and must believe, there is no freedom.

A Free Church in a Free State

In our country we have a free church in a free state. This was a radical dream. We must not lose that dream. We cannot let those who want to wed church and state be victorious. The state should not support the church nor should the church support the state. One should not dictate to the other. As a Christian we should try to influence the state. We should bear witness to the state, but we should not dictate to the state what it should do nor should it dictate to us. Freedom is born in an awareness of a liberating God. That is one of the reasons some people want to stop the study or practice of liberation theology in certain countries. Liberation theology links God with freeing people.

Freedom Is a Continuous Process

Secondly, freedom is never finished. It is always in process of becoming. It is always in danger of being lost. It is always something that we must work at again and again. You and I are very fortunate to live in a country that is free. There are many countries which are not, and we must not take our own freedom for granted.

FREEDOM SYMBOLS

We have numerous symbols for freedom in our country. The Liberty Bell is one of those symbols. That bell was a real bell which was rung early in the life of our country. Now it is just symbolic. The Statue of Liberty is another such symbol. Several years ago it was repaired. Perhaps the decay which had occurred is symbolic of something which is happening within our own country. As with the Statue of Liberty, our own liberty is being eroded away and is in danger of loss. Freedom is always in danger of being lost when the awareness of it significance slowly fades from our memories or when we are unaware of its value. Freedom is always more than a symbol. We need to remember the reality behind the symbol. Freedom needs to be a reality. Freedom is more than something we think about. It needs to permeate our whole being until we are aware that we must constantly fight to sustain its reality.

Do you remember the story of David? Jesus made a reference once to one of David's experiences. Jesus turned to the Scribes and Pharisees and asked, "Do you remember what David did?" (Matthew 12:3ff). When he was fleeing from his enemies and was hungry, he went in the Temple and ate the shewbread from the Table of the Lord. This was the bread which was reserved for the high priests. They would have considered that act a desecration. Then he turned to the priest and asked if they had any weapons of war that he might use to fight his enemies. After thinking for a moment, he responded, "The Sword of Goliath whom you slew in the valley of Blah, behold that is here, wrapped in a cloth behind the ephod. There is none other save that here." (I Samuel 21:1-10). It was the sword of Goliath, of course. It had become only a symbol. It was on display. "There is none like that! Give it to me!" He lifted the sword to take it into battle.

The Liberty Bell, the Statue of Liberty, the Declaration of Independence, and our American flag are all symbols but they are much more. They are more than something to be put on display. The reality behind these symbols needs to remain clearly in our mind lest our freedom be snatched away when we least expect it. These symbols are reminders for us to remain on guard because the battle for freedom is one that is always being waged. We must remain on alert or lose it.

SEEKING GOD'S GUIDANCE

In the beginning of our country, religion played an important role. For five weeks some fifty-five of our countrymen met together trying to draw up a constitution for our new government since they had now written a Declaration of Independence to separate our country from England. Although they worked for five weeks, their efforts were without success. Many felt it was hopeless and were on the verge of adjourning the meeting. Finally, Benjamin Franklin stood up and said, "In this situation of this assembly, groping as it were, in the dark, to find political truth, and scarce able to distinguish it when presented to us, how has it happened, sir, that we have not hitherto once thought of humbly applying to the Father of Lights to illuminate our understanding? We have been assured, sir, in the Sacred writings that 'except the Lord build the house, they labor in vain that build it.' I therefore beg to move that henceforth prayers, imploring the assistance of Heaven and its blessings on our deliberations, be held in this assembly every morning before we proceed to business ... "As they began to ask God to direct them, they quickly began to make progress. John Witherspoon, the chaplain to the Congress and president of the college of New Jersey which later became Princeton, was also one of the signers of the Declaration of Independence. He was a Presbyterian minister.

THE ROLE OF BAPTISTS

Baptists have had a significant role in the pilgrimage of our country and its quest for freedom. The hymn, *My Country 'tis of Thee*, was written in 1832 by a Baptist minister named Samuel Francis Smith. The Pledge of Allegiance to the flag was written in

1892 by Francis Bellamy, a Baptist minister. Baptists have not been afraid to be involved in our country's quest for freedom. In the early stages in the history of our country, a group of Baptist ministers, John Wailer and Lewis Craig and three other dissenters were arrested and put in jail when they tried to preach, in Spotsylvania County, Virginia. They were a part of those who said they wanted no part of an established church. Most of us do not know what the established church is since it doesn't exist in this country. The established church is one which is supported by taxes. Just as we pay taxes to maintain our government, we would be likewise taxed to sustain the church. Although fewer countries actually tax their people for support of the churches today, where this is still done, they are partially controlled by the government and the churches have some input into the government. In most countries where the people are still taxed to support the church, the institutional church is dying. The established church is not the people's church; it is the government's church. We do not want that in our country.

JEFFERSON'S ACT FOR ESTABLISHING RELIGIOUS FREEDOM

One of the crowning achievements which Thomas Jefferson gave our country was the Act for Establishing Religious Freedom. This particular bill Jefferson considered one of the most significant accomplishments of his life. In fact, it is one of the three items which is listed on his grave. When this bill was finally passed in 1786, it stated, "Be it therefore enacted by the General Assembly, that no man shall be compelled to frequent or support any religious worship, place or ministry or whatever, nor shall be enforced, restrained, molested, or burdened in his body or his goods, nor shall otherwise suffer on account of his religious opinions or belief; but that all men shall be free to profess, and by argument to maintain, their opinions in matters of religion, and that the same shall be in no wise diminished, enlarged, or affect their civil capacities." This is a part of the very fabric of our country, and, of all people, especially Baptists should be at the forefront defending the religious rights of all persons.

How can anyone, especially a group of Baptist ministers, say that separation of church and state is not a reality? One of the things that I will never forget when I attended the 1985 Baptist pastor's conference in Dallas, Texas, was hearing a non-Baptist stand up and preach against the separation of church and state and then see him receive a standing ovation from Baptists. It was hard for me to believe that Baptists who had fought and died for separation of church and state could now be so easily dislodged from their foundational belief. We are beginning to lose that basic principle within our denomination.

In place of separation of church and state, many are substituting a civil religion which has now wed the two. Civil religion has tried to claim that this country is a "Christian" nation which can use the government to support whatever kind of religion a select group wants. This, of course, virtually denies religious freedom to non-Christians. I am a Christian and a Baptist and I am proud of both, but I will give a Hindu, a Buddhist, a Muslim, or an atheist his or her right to believe or not believe. That is what religious freedom is — freedom for all, not freedom just for Christians or Jews, but for all persons.

In 1788 John Leland met with James Madison in Orange County, Virginia, under an oak tree near the first church I served as pastor. James Madison persuaded Leland to vote for him with the understanding that upon his election he would see that a Bill of Rights for religious freedom was enacted. Leland got the support of other Baptists so that Madison was elected, and the Bill of Rights with the article for religious freedom was made the law of our land. This is a part of our country's history, and, if we do not know it, we need to understand our past and learn from it.

Freedom is always unfinished, but it is in greater danger of being lost today more than ever before. Many television preachers and other ministers are trying to persuade us that separation of church and state is a myth. Baptists, of all people, need to fight to be certain that religious freedom will continue to be a reality. The signers of the Declaration of Independence put more than words on a piece of paper when they signed their names to that document. The names of John Hancock and John Adams, who did not sign until August 2, were not revealed for six months in hopes that they could get back safely from New Hampshire to their homes in Georgia. The four signers of the Declaration of Independence from the state of New York were very wealthy men who owned fleets of ocean sailing ships. They lost everything they had so our country might be free. How can anyone dare suggest that we deny this kind of freedom today? We as Baptists need to stand tall in this struggle and remember that freedom is always an unfinished battle.

FREEDOM REQUIRES RESPONSIBILITY

Remember, thirdly, that with freedom there always goes responsibility. I think it was Bishop Fulton Sheen who once said that we have a Statue of Liberty off our East Coast and we need a Statue of Responsibility off our West Coast. He is correct. There is no true freedom without responsibility. With our freedom, responsibility is essential to maintain that freedom. With freedom, there needs to be the responsibility to understand what freedom is. Freedom requires the responsibility of its believers to perpetuate it.

Freedom is not easy. It is much easier to be enslaved. Do you remember when Jesus told the Pharisees that he had come to set them free? "What do you mean set us free?" they wondered. "We have always been free. We are Abraham's children." In a sense that was true. To be Abraham's sons they realized that God was the liberating God who had freed them from Egypt. In a spiritual sense, they were always free. But ... they had been in bondage to Babylon, Persia, and, other countries. At the moment when Jesus was speaking to them, they were in bondage to Rome and had been in bondage to Greece. Jesus said, "I will make you free indeed," because the freedom he was giving them was internal. It was a relationship.

THE IMPORTANCE OF VIGILANCE

Jesus' freedom is relational. This is the freedom we have with the Father, and that kind of freedom no one can ever take away from us. We have the freedom of a son or a daughter of God. We are God's children and this relationship is so vital and real that nobody can snatch it away from us even if we are their slaves. In bondage we can still have the kind of freedom which Christ gives. As God's children we are challenged to remember that with our religious freedom goes the responsibility to pass it on to others. We who are free are obligated to teach, preach, and sustain this freedom. If we are not vigilant, we may lose the liberty we cherish so much.

Several years ago an Italian film entitled *General Della Rovere* depicted the work of a resistance movement. The Nazi leaders arrested numerous persons — some of whom were only innocent victims. Unable to identify the resistance leaders, the officer in charge ordered the execution of all those who had been captured.

As the time of the execution drew near, one of those captured cried, "I'm innocent. I did not do anything."

"You did not do anything?" a resistance leader asked.

"No, I did not do anything."

"I do not understand," the resistance leader continued. "Our whole way of life was being destroyed. Minds were being warped; institutions were being subverted; and you did not do anything?"

"No," he said. "I did not do anything."

"Then you deserve to be punished," he responded.

FREEDOM REQUIRES INVOLVEMENT

Too many of us want to be like the man Flip Wilson told about who said that he was a Jehovah's Bystander. He wanted to be a witness, but he did not want to get involved. Too many of us are members of the Jehovah's Bystanders and the Baptist Association of Spectators. We stay in the bleachers. We do not want to get involved. Too many of us stand aloof — stand apart when God has called us to involvement. We are challenged to stand up for freedom, to stand up for those who are oppressed, and to stand up for those who do not agree with us. Jehovah's Witnesses have their freedom today because at some point in the past there were Baptists in our country who were willing to say that although this group differs from us, we will give them the freedom to believe as they will and permit them to worship as they desire.

Can we sit back and do nothing and be spectators and say that we will just do business as usual? Or will we seek to meet the challenge head-on of those who deny religious freedom to all and provide some radical new directions for our people? Freedom is always dangerous. Freedom allows for various viewpoints and different perspectives. It does not call for uniformity but respects diversity. We may not always like or agree with some of the views or ideas that differ from our own. But when real freedom exists, we allow other people to differ with us.

FREEDOM CARRIES ITS DANGERS

Freedom is always dangerous. When we have freedom that means we can have a Ku Klux Klan within our country. They have the freedom to hate Catholics and Jews. Unfortunately, the hatred of the KKK has moved them to want to put some blacks to death. In order to have freedom, individuals have the liberty to hate. But at the same time, others can be loving and strive for ways to care for the needs of those who are oppressed in this country and around the world. Freedom gives room for a Moral Majority, a John Birch Society, or the Salvation Army. It allows for a group to protest the draft. Freedom permits individuals to protest the Iraq War or roll bandages to assist those in combat. There is no true freedom without the opportunity to make choices. Freedom requires us to take a stand or a position on an issue. We have to give others the freedom and right to do the same. Did you know that the results of a recent survey indicate that fifty percent of the citizens in this country do not believe that people who have different religious beliefs from their own should be given freedom to practice their beliefs? That is frightening! It means that we have not taught the principle of freedom very well to our children. The Iraq War was one of the most divisive wars in our country's recent history. Some wanted us to pull out of Iraq soon and others wanted us to stay the course until the battle was won. Good people were on both sides of that conflict.

Gene Owens, who was pastor of Myers Park Baptist Church in Charlotte, North Carolina several years ago, opposed the involvement of our country in the Vietnam War. He felt the war effort was unjust. So he decided to join others across the states who were protesting the war by ringing their church bells. The afternoon after he rang the church bell, a deacon came storming into his study saying, "You had no right to ring our church bell. That is 'our' church bell—not 'your' bell." The next Sunday morning Gene Owens stood up in his pulpit and told the congregation about ringing the church bell and the deacon who had protested his act. "That deacon was right," he declared. "That was not my bell; I did not have any right to ring it. It is the church's bell." Then he reached under the pulpit and pulled out a bell. "But this is my bell," he exclaimed," and I am going to ring it now." He then rang it as loudly as he could. The congregation gave him a standing ovation. He said that week dozens of people gave him bells. The bell became a symbol of his right to take a position and state his own opinion.

Thomas Jefferson once said that the Baptist church is the purest form of democracy. Each person in a Baptist church is a priest before God. The minister cannot tell you exactly what you have to believe. You are a priest before God as I am. Freedom of the pulpit carries with it the responsibility of the pew. In each arena there is a demand for both freedom and responsibility.

FREEDOM WILL ALWAYS HAVE ADVERSARIES

Religious freedom has always had high priests in its hair. Established religion has stayed on the back of religious liberty. It has always had to wage battle against the tyranny of those in power, whether they were kings, queens, lords, or presidents. Religious freedom has constantly fought for its survival against established religion, established government, widespread prejudice, and mass ignorance. If freedom is ever lost, we will be losing one of our most precious possessions. It is always worth the battle to maintain it.

In Harnett County, North Carolina, there is a small church called Barbecue Presbyterian Church. A pistol and a round ball are kept in a small glass case in the church. An interesting story goes with that pistol and ball whether it is true or myth is debatable. Right before the Declaration of Independence was signed, a young Presbyterian minister came from Scotland to serve as pastor of the Barbecue Presbyterian Church. One Sunday he prayed for England, but he also prayed for those in our country who were involved in the revolution and asked God to bless them as well as England. After the service was over, he was met by three loyalists from England. One of them put a pistol against his head and said, 'You see this pistol? If you dare stand in that pulpit and say one more word in support of the revolution, I will put this round ball in your head." He immediately went to the Presbytery and resigned. "I am not a complete fool," he said.

Later in the afternoon, he was walking down the main street of the town and one of his former church members came out of a store cursing. She had not been pleased with her bill. He overheard her and reprimanded her for this offense. She turned to him and said, "Well, preacher, why in the world would you not expect that the devil could do something to a poor little old woman like me if he could make you resign your pulpit in the face of opposition?" He was so shaken by her remarks that the next Sunday he went back to his pulpit and preached a fiery sermon in support of the revolution. After church the three loyalists were waiting for him and sure enough they put a ball in his head and killed him. But to this day in Barbecue Presbyterian Church, there is a ball and a pistol lying in a glass case to remind persons about freedom. They stand as a symbolic reminder, no, as a realistic and concrete image of one man who dared to stand up and lift his voice for freedom.

I hope that we will not lose our freedom as citizens of this country. Let us hold on to our religious freedom. It is a precious heritage. I pray to God that we will always remember its cost, always remember its author, and always remember our own responsibility in maintaining its light. The battle for freedom is always an unending, unfinished battle. Do your part to keep freedom alive!

Loving, Freeing God, forgive us for taking so much for granted and often being willing to do so little. Stimulate our minds with the freedom we have found in Christ. May it always make us free in spirit and in our daily life. Amen.

"WHERE HAVE ALL THE FATHERS GONE?"

LUKE 15:11-32
PSALM 78:1-7

I want to reword an old folk song from Pete Seeger:

> Where have all the fathers gone, long time missing?
> Where have all the fathers gone, long time ago? Where
> have all the fathers gone?
> They've lost their halos one by one;
> When will we ever learn? When will we ever learn?

In our country today 40 percent of American children will go to bed tonight without fathers living in the home. Nearly 50 percent of the children in America will spend a substantial amount of their lifetime apart from their fathers.[25] David Blankenhorn has written a provocative book entitled *Fatherless America*. In it he is challenging America to realize that "the absence of fathers in our country is the most urgent social problem we have."[26] One of the great tragedies in our land today is the idea that fathers are no longer important. Blankenhorn's book challenges that thesis.

On September 21, 1992, on the season premiere of the sitcom, *Murphy Brown*, our country experienced an important cultural moment. Murphy Brown had decided to give birth to her child outside of marriage. She stated that she would raise her child without a father. She would be a single mother by choice. When many voices across our land criticized the show, including the Vice-President of the United States, Dan Quayle, for "mocking the importance of fathers," a national controversy erupted. The Vice-President was ridiculed and this season premier rebuked him for his "unfair remarks about the necessity of fathers."

That same day the *Washington Post* ran an article on the front page, seeming, almost to be promoting the episode, entitled "Conventional Family Value Is Being Reevaluated." The journalist wrote, in a cheerleading fashion, for the message of the show, that "a searching reevaluation by social scientists had now demonstrated that the consequences of absent fathers from children have been overstated and that, as a result, the conventional two parent household may be far less critical to the healthy development of children than previously believed."[27] That assumption is what Dr. Blankenhorn is challenging in his book. Some research scientists, like Frank L. Mott, are declaring that in child rearing we really do not need two parents – one is sufficient.[28] The assumption is that a father's absence from the home is not a major factor in the development of a child.

---

25 David Blankenhorn, Fatherless America (New York: Basic Books, 1995), 1.
26 *Ibid.*
27 Malcolm Gladwell "Conventional Family's Value Is Being Reevaluated" Washington Post, September 21, 1992.
28 Blankenhorn, 70.

THE MISSING FATHERS

There is no question today that in many families there is a missing father. The father is often absent because of his job, or he is absorbed in the television set. Some children know their fathers primarily from the perspective of "Don't bother me, I am busy," or "Run along now, I've got too much to do," or "I'm sorry, I can't talk to you now." Maybe that is what led Billy Sunday to say many years ago, "If there is a good mother in a family, any old stick will do for a father." Unfortunately, that is the notion that is prevalent today. Many fathers are missing, absorbed in something else. They are simply not present for their families.

DEAD-BEAT DADS

We also have what are called "dead-beat dads." These are fathers who have either abandoned or divorced their families and do not support them in any way whatsoever. *Newsweek* magazine several years ago had a front page, framed with a Wanted poster, entitled "Dead-beat Dads Wanted for Failure To Pay Child Support." A young girl in The Child Guidance Center in Akron, Ohio, wrote an imaginary letter to her father:

> Dear Dad:
>
> I wish you the worst Father's Day ever. And if you don't pay, you don't get love. Oh, yeah, by the way, my mom makes, less money than you. I hate you.[29]

Dead-beat dads! These are fathers who do not support their families financially. They bring a child into the world and then abandon him or her.

VISITING DADS

There are also those we can call "visiting dads." These are fathers who are products of divorce. These fathers may genuinely

---

29 *Ibid*, 125.

want to care for their children but can only see them occasionally. They stop by when they can or at times which are allotted. In 1993, I, like many of you, saw the movie, *Mrs. Doubtfire*. Robin Williams played the role of a father who loved his children, but the court denied him custody and greatly restricted his visitation rights. In a desperate move he dressed up like a woman and was hired to be the children's nanny. It is an entertaining movie. One of the most interesting things to me in the movie was what many people seemed to miss. The father, Daniel Hilland, became acceptable when he became a mother. There are many in our society who are trying to remove the father from a family. They declare that the mother alone is sufficient.

It Could Be Worse

There are others who are saying that the family unit can do without a father because with one "it could be worse." They declare that no father at all may be better than some of the sorry types of persons who are fathers. Ann Lamont wrote an article on the "Could Be Worse" situation about the fatherlessness in the *New York Times*. "I would give anything for Sam (her son) to have a great father." This is a woman who is single with no father in the picture for the child. "But I will not risk giving him a bad one. It is better to have no father than to have one of those mean, lazy men who couldn't even bring up a houseplant."[30]

A Needed Father Model

We have all kinds of disturbing images of fathers that are being expounded in our land today. For those in our congregation today who are single, female parents and are seeking to raise your child alone, or to those whose father is dead and you have to raise your child by yourself, I am saying to you and to those who are fathers, the same message, the father is essential. We need some father model in every family. For those who have no father, then you need a surrogate or a substitute. That substitute may come in

---

30 Ibid, 70.

the form of a grandfather, a teacher, a coach, a minister, a scout leader, a Boys and Girls Club leader, or a friend. Every child needs some male who can model for the child what it is like to be a man. This is not to minimize all the wonderful gifts that women have. I affirm them all. But women are not men and men are not women. We need both. For a child to develop properly, he or she needs a masculine image. I think we need to affirm that. In some communities where there is an absence of fathers, Fathers Clubs and MAD DADS Clubs have been formed.

In Blankenhorn's book he offers 12 proposals to counter the crisis. I don't have time to tell you about them this morning, but they are all helpful. His first proposal is the following pledge: "Many people today believe that fathers are unnecessary. I believe the opposite. I pledge to live my life according to the principle that every child deserves a father, that marriage is the pathway to effective fatherhood; that part of being a good man means being a good father; and that America needs more good men."[31] He believes that every piece of domestic legislation that Congress would seek to enact needs to be considered from the viewpoint of whether it will strengthen or weaken the institution of marriage.[32] He would encourage professional athletes to organize a public service campaign on the importance of fatherhood."[33]

THE ORIGIN OF FATHER'S DAY

This is Father's Day. Do you know the origin of Father's Day? A woman named Mrs. John Bruce Dodd was sitting in church on Mother's Day, 1909, in Spokane, Washington. After the sermon which honored mothers, Mrs. Dodd thought that we ought to have something to honor our fathers as well. She took her idea to the ministerial association. They liked the suggestion and chose June, the month of Mrs. Dodd's father's birthday. The mayor of Spokane, Washington, heard about the idea and he liked it. He issued

---

31   Ibid, 226.
32   Ibid, 231.
33   Ibid, 233.

a formal Father's Day proclamation. The governor of the State of Washington heard about it and he set the third Sunday in June for observance in the State of Washington. In 1924 Grover Cleveland, President of the United States, recommended it as a national holiday. This day was set aside because one woman thought that fathers needed special recognition. This morning I want to raise a banner and wave that flag: Fathers are important! Don't listen to those who tell us today that fathers are unnecessary. I know we have a lot of homes without fathers. What we need to do is to find substitutes and some ways to get healthy father images before girls and boys.

A DEFINITION OF FATHER

What is the definition of a father? Have you ever looked up the definition of father in your dictionary? Look the definition up in a large dictionary. You will discover many. Some contain fifteen or more. Some of these images have Latin, Sanskrit, German, French, Dutch or Irish roots. About middle way down you will find this etymological root — the father is the source or prototype. The father is the source of strength or the one from whom the family draws strength.

Our Lord, Jesus Christ, when he chose a word to describe God, He said "Father." Jesus told us to pray, "Our Father." Again and again Jesus used references to God as Father. One time he used the most intimate of all expressions, "Abba," or "Daddy." When he was hanging on the cross dying, Jesus cried, "Father, into Your hands, I commit my spirit." One of the most beautiful parables which Jesus told is the one about the loving father. I think we can learn some wonderful lessons from this parable on how to try to be better fathers. Let me suggest a few lessons this morning.

THE IMPORTANCE OF ACCEPTANCE

The first thing that I see in this parable is acceptance. The father accepted both of his sons. He gave them freedom to find their own ways. You remember, in the play and movie, *Fiddler on The Roof*, where the father is musing to himself one day that he did not realize that his children had grown older. Tevye and his wife began to sing "Sunrise, Sunset." Every father needs to look at his family and see what direction they are going as they grow older. Children grow fast and we may miss a part of that process.

I am very appreciative of the fact that my father accepted me and gave me freedom to become myself. When I was a freshman in college and wanted to go to California to work one summer, my parents struggled with my wish. They were not sure they wanted their young son to go all the way to California and be on his own at such a young age. But they trusted and accepted me and gave me the freedom to grow. I spent a summer in California and did home mission work. I am a better person for that. And my father gave me that freedom.

When our son decided after one year of college that he wanted to drop out of school for a while, that was difficult for a guy who had spent all of his years going straight through college and seminary like I did. But his mother and I accepted him for who he was, and he went out west and worked for a while. Later Bill came back to college and completed his education. We have to learn to accept our children for who they are and let them know that they are loved. The father in this parable did that.

GIVE AFFIRMATION

Secondly, the father affirmed his sons. He affirmed them for the gifts each had. That didn't mean that the father approved of everything they did. He certainly didn't approve of everything his young son did. But, he affirmed him as a part of the family when he left and when he returned. He told his elder son that "all I have is yours." Both of them received their father's love and affirmation because they were his sons and were important to him. Our family needs to have our priority. Blankenhorn is insisting that today's fathers need to learn to put their families first.

John Killinger tells about a friend of his who is a Seventh-day Adventist pastor named Gary Patterson in Walla Walla, California. He was pastor of a 2,500 member church, one of the leading churches in his denomination. He received an invitation to become president of the Kansas Conference of Seventh-day Adventists, a prestigious position in his denomination. He always wanted to be a conference president and he was elected. He came home at lunchtime and shared this decision with his family. His wife and daughter were thrilled. But his son, Geoff, was not present. That night when they gathered for the meal, Geoff came in all enthusiastic because he had been the flag bearer for the 8th Grade graduation exercise. He declared, "Do you know what this means? Next year I will be assured of victory in the student election. It is guaranteed." Geoff's mother left the table crying. And his father got up and followed her and said, "It's okay, honey. I guess Geoff needs to be president of the 8th grade more than I need to be president of the Kansas Conference." The matter was settled and he declined the offer. That rarely happens, folks. More fathers need to realize the importance of their family and affirm them with the decisions we make in our lives.

BE AVAILABLE

Thirdly, we need to let them know that we are available. They need time and attention from us. The father gave time to both his sons. A small girl brought a picture that she had received an A on in class one day and showed it to her father. She said, "This is a picture of our family and look dad, I got an A on it." The father looked at the picture and he saw the family sitting in the den and suddenly he realized, as he looked at the picture, that he was not in it. For you see, he was never at home. He was always gone. He was always at work, always away on a trip, always somewhere else. We need to find time to be available to our family. We need to find the time to bathe our children when they are small, to read stories to them, to play with them, and to touch them, so they know we care and love them.

Dr. Charlie Shedd said he was rushing to his church for a committee meeting one night and his little daughter, Karen, stopped him and said, "Daddy, read me a story." He started to give the usual excuse and say, "I don't have time." But, instead, he sat down with her and took three minutes and read the story. When he closed the book, he said, "We will have to come back later and see how the story ends." Karen looked at him and said, "Oh, Daddy, I know how it ends. Mother reads that story to me all the time." All she wanted to know was whether or not she was more important to him than a stupid old meeting. We need to be available to our family.

LEARN TO COMMUNICATE

We need also, fourthly, to learn to communicate more effectively. In this parable the father takes time to talk with both of his sons. He was willing to engage in conversation with both of them. Often a child or a wife in a family will cry out to the father or husband, "Talk to me, listen to me." Children long to have a father who will take the time to listen. Take time to listen to their problems, listen to their hopes, and listen to their dreams. Communication is essential. We need to open our ears and be attentive.

GIVE ENCOURAGEMENT

Continue further with me in the fifth place. Fathers need to give encouragement. In our parable the father encouraged one of his sons to venture on his own. He encouraged his other son to know that he loved him no matter what he did. Fathers need to encourage their children and say to them, "I love you and I am there for you."

Our son-in-law, John, told us about the time he had been at Virginia Military Institute for several months. He had a rigorous schedule. He attended classes and was a part of the military unit. He called home and told his father, "Come and get me, I want to come home." His father said, "No, son. This is your bed you have chosen to lie on it and you must now follow through." His father continued to encourage him. John stuck with it and graduated later from VMI. Today he is an engineer because of the encouragement of his father.

There are times we feel like we want to give up and quit, because the going gets hard. We need fathers who will encourage us, lift us up and stand with us through the difficult times in life.

Give Unconditional Love

Go further and note in the sixth place that we need unconditional love from our fathers. In the parable when the prodigal son came back home, his father received him with open arms and embraced him. The father was not approving of everything his son did. But he loved his son unconditionally, because he was his father. He was still a part of the family. But the father also loved his other "prodigal son" who stayed at home just as well. Unconditional love offers forgiveness, acceptance and support.

Two little boys were talking one day and one of them had done something that was wrong. The other one said to him, "Daddy is not going to love you if you do that." The boy's father overheard his son and he came over and hugged them both. He said, "Son, your daddy will love you when you do something that is good and he will feel proud. But your father will still love you when you do something bad. I will be sad, but I will love you all the time."

God's love is unconditional. Our love as a father needs to reach out to our son, daughter, or spouse and say to them, "**I** love you and **I** am there for you."

Model Your Love

And then going a step further, observe in the seventh place that a father needs to model his love. There was a little sign hanging in a shop that read: "The best way a father can show his love for his children is to love their mother." Not bad! Fathers need to model their love. We need to model it by the time and attention we give our children and our wife. We need to help our children learn things, explore new territory, find themselves and understand life. We model our love by spending time playing games with them, fishing, hunting, playing tennis, swimming, hiking, or sitting down playing dolls with them, etc. Whatever it is, we give them time and attention because we care and love them. We model love and don't just talk about it.

In one of our congregations there was a man who was the manager of the electric company in our community. He got a number of job offers to go other places because he was an outstanding individual. He and his wife both told us that they had made a decision not to leave our community until their children had graduated from high school. They said that they thought that our church and community were wonderful places to bring up their children.

Friends, that is modeling love. Do we really put our children first? If we do, we will seek to do the very best for them before we even consider careers or anything else. That is not easy to do.

BE A SPIRITUAL LEADER

And then, lastly, the father needs to be the spiritual leader — the teacher of values, and the teacher of high principles in the family. He should be the one who teaches his children their boundaries and limits in life, as well as their ideals and goals. A good father will try to teach his children to go to church, not just by saying, "go," but by taking them. He will be there with them. He will set the example that Sunday School and worship are important, because he will be there with them.

We wonder sometimes why children quit going to Sunday School and church. Guess where they learn that! The father in the family ought to be the example that church and spiritual matters are important. Let the father model so his children will follow.

When we lived in Bristol, Tennessee, we had a deep snow fall one winter and I had gone out in the yard to play in the snow with our children. As I was walking along across the yard I looked behind me, I saw both of my children, Catherine and Bill, who were very small at that time, following me. Catherine yelled and said, "Daddy, we are walking in your steps." As I took a step in the snow, they would step in my impression in the snow behind me as they followed along. You know, I have never forgotten that image. "Daddy, we are walking in your steps." And so they do!

Fathers, you will set examples again and again for your children. We ought to set good examples in our values, in our worship and in everything that is important. Let us as fathers teach our children so they will know that we love God and that we love them and we want them to be the very best that they can be. Where have all the fathers gone? I hope that we will seek to make fathers in this church, in our community and across our country essential to the health of our families. Let each father seek to be the very best father he can be wherever he is.

> *Loving Father, we acknowledge that those of us who are fathers are not what we should be. But, Lord, we want to be the kind of father that will make you proud, that will serve You most effectively and will make our families better. Give us the courage and the insight in how to be those kinds of men. Through Christ, our Lord, we pray. Amen.*

"The Gospel Addresses Our Work"

Psalm 90:16-17
Matthew 20:1-16

Over one hundred years ago, in 1882, the Knights of Labor, as they were called then, asked that a day be set aside to honor laboring persons. In 1894, Congress authorized Labor Day as a national holiday, and we have continued to celebrate it since that time.

If you work to a normal retirement age of 65, or if you have already worked until that time, averaging about eight hours a day, 40 hours a week, more or less, in your lifetime, you will put in about 100 thousand hours working in your job. That is a lot of time! And it is a long time especially if you find your work boring, frustrating, dull, and without meaning, which a lot of people say is the way they view their job. This is a great tragedy.

Edward Harris observed several years ago:

It is abundantly clear that unless our religion can address itself to our work with powerful and illuminating insight, our religion will be out of touch with a large important part of our life and we will be hard put to escape the damaging charge of irrelevancy.

For many, there is no relationship between work and religion. The divorce has been made clean and separate. Persons seem to say: "I do what I want to do in my work, and religion is something I do for a few moments in church on Sunday." But I do not think that can be true if our religion is meaningful.

A Day's Work

Suppose you were a hard working man centuries ago who was awakened by the sun as it began to rise and set its glow against the sky. This day looked like the kind of day you could get a job. It was late August. You could feel the hot breeze blowing its breath upon you as you lay upon your pallet in your mud hut. Quickly you rush down to the marketplace, and sure enough the owner of the vineyard is looking for someone to work in his vineyard. The owner knows that the September rains are coming soon, and he must harvest his crop while the weather is still good. You are hired at six o'clock, the beginning hour of the day for a Jewish man in the first century. You feel fortunate because by being hired at six in the morning that means that you can get a full day's wage, if you can work until six o'clock that night. A normal working day was from six until six.

Soon you are working in the field in the sun. It is hotter than you thought even that early in the morning. You notice that the owner goes off to the square and soon brings back some other men at nine o'clock to join you working in the field. At noon he goes to the city again and brings back some more workers. At three he returns with even more workers. But the owner notices that the grapes are still not all harvested, so he goes back to the city even at the late hour of five, which is only one hour before the working day is to be over, and brings back some other men to labor with you. At last it's time to get paid. You are to be paid as the custom is at the end of each day and not at the end of the week. You had been promised that you would be paid a denarius, 24 cents, for this day's work, which was a working man's wage for a day's labor. You notice, to your joy, that the boss paid the last man, who came to work only one hour before quitting, a denarius. You think, "Ah-ha, that means that if he only worked for an hour and received that much, surely I'm going to get a whole lot more."

The owner could have avoided the problem that followed if he had simply paid those who had begun work at 6:00 a.m. first. Your heart slips just a bit as you notice that the man who came at three is paid the same thing. Then the man who came at twelve also receives a denarius. As you stick out your hand the owner gives you the same thing he has paid the rest and by now you are really mad. Having worked in the scorching sun all day long, you say to your boss: "What is this? Why don't you give me more? I have worked here all day long in this blazing sun, and that rascal who sat around in the marketplace most of the day and worked only one hour, got as much as I did. It is not fair." The owner says: "Friend, why are you jealous if I am generous? If I feel that this man should have a full day's wage for only one hour's work, why should you feel that I have been unfair to you?"

In Jesus' parable found in Matthew 20:1-16 we note that this obviously is not an economic tract focusing on hourly wages. It is a theological statement. This parable is not concerned so much with equal work or equal pay. There are, however, some insights within this parable and a central truth that can tell us something about how to relate our work and our faith. This parable may force us to look at our work on a deeper level.

THE IMPORTANCE OF THE MARKETPLACE

One of the facts we need to understand in this story, is that Jesus did not intend to depict the men who were sitting around the marketplace as lazy. This was the place where individuals were supposed to go when they did not have a regular job or trade of some kind or did not own land. The marketplace was the spot for workers to gather who wanted to work. Maybe a new beatitude could be coined in which we might say, "Blessed are those who give others work because they give them self-respect." It is one of the unfortunate myths of our society, especially in this country, that most people who are not working really do not want to work. Studies have demonstrated that this is not true. We have freeloaders in society, but most people want the self-respect that comes from having a job. Those who are in the business structures of society and are able to offer jobs to others should see that as a part of their Christian responsibility. To be able to offer work to those who need it is a worthy responsibility. All persons have the right to work and the right to a fair wage and the dignity and self-respect which accompanies it.

Our Attitude Affects Our Work

It is interesting also to observe the attitude that is reflected in the men who had worked all day. Notice the anger which one man feels toward another when he thinks he should have received more wages and he does not. Think about how often that happens in our work relationships today. People, of course, labor for different reasons. Sometimes a person works purely for money alone. It is always a great tragedy when a person is engaged in work only for money and sees nothing deeper than that in it. In this parable one man becomes angry because the owner seeks to pay another the same wage for less work than he had done.

In our society today, there is no question that one's attitude toward his or her work often indicates the kind of work we do. What many produce is reflected by the kind of attitude that goes into their work. You may have heard about a man named Sam who left his job. Somebody asked another employee, "Who did they fill the vacancy with when Sam left?" The guy responded, "Huh, Sam didn't leave no vacancy when he left." There are a lot of folks who are only filling their jobs and when they leave, they do not leave a vacancy. They have never really put much into their job while they have had it.

The Proper Motivation for Work

Our work requires of us responsibility and commitment to do the very best that we can while we engage in it. A few of us can be like the president of a university one time who told his friends, "They pay me for doing what I would gladly do free if I could afford it." It would be a delight if all of our jobs could be like that, but we know that is not always true. We need, nevertheless, to press into our lives some sense of proper motivation for our reason for doing the kind of work we do. It is not always easy in our kind of society to talk about the joy of working because some of our work is indeed grinding, grueling, and difficult. All work is not enjoyable and easy.

When I was in college, I worked for several years as a custodian. My job was to clean the biology and chemistry labs, the Chapel, and classrooms in an administration building. I can't say I always enjoyed that job, but I tried to keep in my mind a sense of the higher purpose and motivation for doing this particular job. Somehow as I cleaned the chapel, the biology or physics labs, I tried to envision that I, in some small way, was contributing to the health and education of others so that they might have a clean, safe place in which to learn. Many students often have to do jobs that have no real meaning for the moment other than providing money to help pay for their education. But the larger goal gives meaning to the work in the present.

Work to the Best of Your Ability

Through this parable, Jesus teaches that in the sight of God there is a sense in which all work has a sameness with God, if it is done properly and done with a sense of honor and dignity. Unfortunately, we often assume that there is only one kind of good work, and then we begin to categorize those who do menial work with their back or hands. Many do not regard that kind of labor as highly as that which is done with the mind or what is done in a chair behind a desk. But each laborer contributes his or her place and part in the total well-being of society and each makes an important contribution.

Karl Barth, the famous theologian, goes so far as to say that in the church's ministry, it does not matter whether one is the pastor or the custodian. In the eyes of God, if each does his work to the very best of his ability, that work before God is equal.[34]

Some See Work as a Curse

One of the unfortunate things in our society is that sometimes people view work as a curse. Many believe that work is the curse that God placed upon us at the fall of Adam and Eve. (Genesis 3:14-19)

In a *Peanuts* comic Snoopy provides us an image of our feeling. He is on his dog house sleeping.

Lucy comes along and says, "Wake up, you stupid beagle, it's five o'clock."

He says, "Oh, no!"

"If we're going to skate in the Christmas show, we've got to practice and practice and practice!" she says.

"While the stars are still out?" Snoopy asks.

"Stop complaining . . . Getting up early in the morning is good for you . . ." Lucy declares.

"I hope it's good for me," Snoopy mourns, "because it's killing me."

There are a lot of people who feel that their work is a curse, but they do it to get by even if it kills them.

But this is not the biblical attitude toward work. When you read the Genesis account carefully, you find that man was placed in the garden to till the garden before the curse was given. (Genesis 2:15) Man is set to work naming the animals and caring for the garden. Man and woman are involved in work as co-creators with

---

34 Karl Barth, "Files of Commission I, World Council of Churches, Geneva, first draft of Barth's article for The Universal Church in God's Design," quoted in *The Realm of Redemption* by J. Robert Nelson (Greenwich: The Seabury Press, 1951), 145.

the Creator. Work is not a curse but a blessing. Work is a gift to us from God who invites us to engage with God as God's workers in the world. We are given an opportunity to share in the Creator's work. We participate with God in the continuation of creation. This does not mean that our work will always be easy or that everything we do is without difficulty.

Even for our eternal God, work is not always easy. As God works with creation – man, woman, and the rest of the universe – problems arise from the freedom given to creatures and creation. Wherever there is freedom, even for God, there has to be some difficulty that creation is constantly giving God. But God has created us with the freedom to be co-laborers in the universe.

GOD'S GRACE IS EXTRAVAGANT

When we reflect on this parable and the way the owner responds to the various lengths of time the men work, we want to declare quickly that it seems so unfair for him to be like this. One of the central truths that comes from this parable is that, like the owner in this parable, God is extravagant in generosity. God does not love some of us more because some of us work harder, or because some of us have superior minds, or superior backs, or superior jobs. God's love to us is an expression of God's grace and is not dependent upon our own efforts to earn it. This parable affirms a God of love who truly extends his graciousness and favor toward us. God still loves us and will continue to love us. Our attitude toward God cannot destroy that love.

There is an old legend about the witch of Alexandria who used to walk down the ancient streets and carry in one hand a blazing torch and in the other a bucket of water. She exclaimed that she wanted to burn up heaven and extinguish the flames of hell so people will love God only because of who He is and not for reward or fear of punishment.

Our desire to love and serve God should be based on our response to God's love and grace. Our work should be a reflection of our love of God. We labor with God in our world, not because we are seeking to do something for recognition from God or others, or because of some kind of awful sense of fear. Instead, we labor and serve out of the love and commitment that we have toward God, the Creator.

Use the Opportunities You Have

It is also interesting to observe in this parable that the men worked with the opportunities which they had. "Why are you standing in the marketplace idle?" they were asked. "Lord, no one has given us work to do," they respond. Some people do not have greater opportunities because they simply have not had doors open for them. Sometimes they have not prepared themselves so that the doors might open. But whatever doors of opportunity open before us, small or large, each of us is to use the abilities and talents he or she has to the very best of one's ability. When we labor as best we can where we are God sees that work and says that it is good.

On occasion, I have watched the bricklayers and other construction workers as they have worked on church buildings where I have been pastor. When I was in high school, I used to work as a bricklayer's helper and carpenter's helper and remember well what that kind of manual labor involved. I have often wondered if the men who were engaged in that work on our church buildings were able to see something of a higher vision in what they were doing. They were doing more than just laying bricks and sawing boards. They were building a church for the worship of God. I hope they saw that.

A part of the vision of our work needs to be the recognition, that in some way, the work that I am doing is contributing to the betterment of humanity and to the glory of God. I know it is hard to see that in some jobs because they are difficult and demanding. If one works in a factory, for example, and all you do is turn or assemble one small part, then you need to see the greater part or higher goal for which your labor is but one of many parts. Hopefully, you see not just the part that you make but the refrigerator or automobile or spaceship, or whatever it is to which you are contributing a part. We need to see how we help other people or how we give greater service for humankind. When we lose sight of the higher goal, our work does become drudgery. To see our labor only in a particular moment is to lose the vision of the greater wholeness and the opportunity it affords us to share in wider service.

Years ago there were two women who wanted to serve as missionaries. Both of them prepared themselves and they were approved by the mission board. When it came time to be appointed, one of them went on to her foreign field of service. She served faithfully as a missionary in a distant country, and married another missionary. They had children, and they served all their lives on the mission field. The other young woman began to reappraise her situation. If she went to the mission field, what would her parents do? Both of her parents were elderly, and had no source of income other than what she could provide for them. She decided that she could not go to the mission field and leave her parents alone. So she stayed home, supported and cared for her parents until they died.

When they died, she was forty-seven years old, and no mission board would appoint her then. She served faithfully in her local church and in her community. She served wherever she could and offered her gifts to God. Now which one received greater recognition in the eyes of God? Oh, I know what we say. But in the eyes of God, which is the greater service? Are those who serve as missionaries on the foreign fields the most committed? Can one not take seriously his or her responsibilities in the place where he or she is and labor for God there?

WE CANNOT SEPARATE THE SACRED AND SECULAR

All of us do not have the same opportunities or the same abilities. If you give the very best to God with the gifts you have, in God's sight all work is of equal worth. Whether you farm, build houses, cook, or work as a teacher, executive, minister or missionary, if you serve faithfully, no one's work is judged more important or more sacred to God. God does not measure his response by what we deserve but by our needs, ability and commitment. We serve

God and labor in our work, not for reward or recognition from God. We cannot separate the sacred and secular, because God is involved in our work and in our worship. We worship through our work and work through our worship.

In a small Moravian church, the congregation uses a workbench as their communion table. During the week, one of the men in the church uses it as his carpenter's workbench, but, then, on Sunday it is brought into the church and used as the place where they commune and fellowship with God. Should not all of our work be like that? Through our work, we serve, minister, and worship in God's name.

OUR COMPENSATION IS GOD'S COMPANIONSHIP

The God, who is the Creator, loves us and seeks to have companionship with us. Our only real compensation for our labor, we are told through this parable, is God's companionship. Jesus told this parable right after Peter and the others had wanted to know what rewards they would receive for following him. For those who labor long and hard, this parable might sound unfair. Jesus declared that one could not say that only those who labored long count with God. We cannot pile up merit before God or win God's favor. Our relationship to God is not purchased; it is a gift. God gives out of gracious love to us. God's love is not something we can earn but is an expression of extravagant love toward us. Our compensation is God's companionship. There is an ancient prayer that states that truth this way: "Teach us to labor and not ask for any reward, save that of knowing that we do thy will." Rudyard Kipling wrote years ago:

> And only the master shall praise us and only the master shall blame. And no one shall work for money, no one shall work for fame. But each for the joy of working and each in his separate star shall draw the things as he sees them for the God of things as they are.[35]

---

35 Rudyard Kipling, "L'ENVOI," *Masterpieces of Religious Verse*, edited by James Dalton Morrison (New York: Harper & Brothers Publishers, 1948), 602.

It is God who is generous and loving. God is extravagant. If we are concerned because some brother comes into the Kingdom late and is loved graciously by God, the problem is not with God but with us. If we are jealous because a sister or brother is received by God when he or she is elderly and experiences the grace of God, then the problem is not with God but with us. We respond, hopefully, to God's extravagant goodness toward others not be-grudgingly but with thankfulness that not only they but we have not been treated, as we deserve but according to the graciousness of God. Through Christ we have experienced the great generosity of the God who has so loved us that He has given us His son.

Oh Gracious God, sometimes we get our values twisted around and we think it is by our own efforts that we have rights before you. Make us mindful that it is because of your generous and extravagant love that we have experienced grace. May that experience continue to grow. Amen

"On Not Losing Your Vision"

Numbers 13:25-33
Matthew 17:14-20

In life there are two basic ways of seeing. One is positive; the other is negative. One perspective sees only the darkness; the other is able to see the beginning of dawn. The one is able to see only defeat; the other is able to see victory. One is only able to see despondency; the other is able to see hope. One is able to see only a pile of rubble; another sees materials from which to begin rebuilding. One sees a dead-end street; another sees opportunity to make a new road. One person sees a glass, half-empty; the other sees it half-full. How do you see? Do you have negative or positive vision in life? Most of the time, when we talk with someone, we can tell rather quickly how they see, because they reveal almost immediately in their conversation whether they see life with negative eyes or positive vision.

NEGATIVE VISION

The two stories which we read from the Scripture today speak about negative and positive vision. Let us look for a moment at these stories. Notice, first of all, that there, is a great deal of negative vision which they project toward life. The children of Israel, according to this Old Testament selection, had moved to the very edge of the Promised Land. They had traveled for forty years in the wilderness. Now Moses sent some spies to go into the land that lay before them to see what it was like. Twelve men, one from each tribe, traveled for forty days through the land, probably moving in the darkness of night, and scurrying about here and there in the day time, trying not to be seen as they observed the land and people who lived there. They discovered that, compared to the desert where they had been for forty years, this was a very fertile land. It was indeed flowing with milk and honey. Their report pictured the land as being fantastically rich with promise. To prove their point, they returned with pomegranates, figs, and a large bunch of grapes swinging on a long pole. The great luxury of the land could be seen by all.

Caleb was the spokesman. He declared: "Let us go up at once and occupy the country; we are well able to conquer it." Joshua sided with him, but the other ten were reluctant and exclaimed: "Wait a minute, these people look like giants to us. They are the sons of Anak, the 'long-necked ones." Goliath, some scholars believe, may have been a descendant of this group. These men looked gigantic to these former slaves. "We look like grasshoppers to them," they cried. Their attitude is astounding. God's presence had been with them through all of their years of wandering and now, as they get ready to enter the Promised Land, they take a tremendously negative view. Fear had overtaken them, and their enemy seemed like large giants. "We are grasshoppers," they said. Grasshoppers are helpless, feeble, and have a low perspective toward life.

A GRASSHOPPER VIEW OF LIFE

We all know something about the grasshopper view of life, don't we? Some of us, if we are older, can recall those days when we were very small and everybody did look like giants to us. Remember the days in elementary school when you looked up at all of the giants around you, until you yourself began to grow up and you became a giant to someone else. It is amazing how often in life we see whatever obstacles arise before us as giants to be conquered. We feel as insignificant as grasshoppers, and a negative view slowly begins to permeate everything we do in our reaction to life. Instead of the highest goal possible, we reach toward the lowest maximum we can achieve as we seek to make our contribution in life. With this negative view toward life, we try to get by with the very least that we can. We often do this in our marriage. We do it in our church life and in our business life. We take this approach in almost every area of our life. We aim at the lowest common denominator and live out this negative view toward life. We become satisfied with the least we can do and do not reach for the highest within us.

Professors and teachers in school detect this perspective from students rather quickly. When they assign a paper to students, hands go up and the student asks: "Does it have to be ten pages? Can it be less?" Many students would not dream of writing a paper longer than the minimum page. "Does it have to have a bibliography?" "Does it need footnotes?" Most want everything else excluded so they can do the least amount of work required. Many do not have the desire to do the kind of research that will make them the best informed student they need to be, but seek, instead, the avenue which requires the least amount of effort. There is no excitement or enthusiasm for the subject. Too often that is the same approach we take toward our religion. It is often our approach toward marriage, parenting, and unfortunately, toward too much of life. The desire to get by with the least we can do is a negative attitude which is reflected often in our words and deeds.

Charlie Brown came walking out of his house to feed Snoopy one day. Snoopy was lying on top of his doghouse.

Charlie Brown said to him, as he poured his dog food, "This food has been no trouble at all for me to fix for you today. It is just dry cereal and all I had to do was pour some water in it and it is ready to eat."

Snoopy looked at it and, after Charlie Brown walked away, he said, "I'd rather be worth a little trouble."

The things in life which are really worthwhile usually require a little trouble. But too often we give way to the negative view and not the positive and seek to do the least we can.

Lost Their Vision of the Power of God

Notice, secondly, in these stories that these people had lost their vision of the power of God. In some ways it is almost astounding that the children of Israel would have that happen to them when they had lived daily with God going before them as a pillar of fire. Through this pillar of fire, God's presence had been made known. Now as they are getting ready to go into the Promised Land, they have forgotten about this presence and now they see only the giants which loom before them and have forgotten about God.

Look briefly at the New Testament story.

The transfiguration has just taken place. Jesus has been transfigured before some of his disciples. Moses and Elijah appeared there on the mountain with Jesus. When Jesus came back down from the mountain following the transfiguration, he found a young lad there who was possessed by a demon. He discovered that his disciples were unable to cure the boy, and he said: "Oh you of little faith." Sometimes we have lots of faith on the mountaintops of life, but, when we come down into the valleys where there are difficulties and problems, our faith seems to be inadequate to sustain us.

Raphael, in a marvelous painting of this scene, shows Jesus on the mountaintop transfigured with Moses and Elijah. The disciples with him are lying on the ground in an attitude of deepest awe. Down in the valley below, one can see the other disciples surrounded by a crowd of people, with the father and his young tormented son whom the disciples are helpless to cure. Some are pointing up toward the mountaintop where Christ is and where they will draw their source of strength.

Why Did They Lose Their Vision?

Why do you suppose that the Israelites and the disciples responded in such a negative way?

They Were Afraid

Well, for one thing, they simply were afraid. The Israelites saw the giants in the Promised Land, and they were fearful of confronting them. The giants seemed too formidable to them. We, too, know something of these kinds of fears when we seek to move forward in life. We see individuals who are too threatening to us. Danger seems to lurk at us from many sides. The obstacles appear too difficult, so we fall back in great fear. We can't face the challenge. It seems impossible. As young people, you have fears about college or what lies ahead of you.

Years ago this church had a vision of a great building through which it might serve and minister in this community. You built that building and it has drawn people to use it and to the church itself. Some are discouraged by the debt, although the church is meeting it well. Others wonder if we will ever be able to build the children's building. They are afraid and wonder if we can possibility be the church we were. In the course of the years, it is amazing how some lost their vision and slipped away and did not remain because fears of all kinds began to creep into their thinking. "Can we pay for it?" "Can we do this?" "Can we do the other?" Soon fear began to take over, instead of the vision which had guided them. But others saw the possibilities and trusted God.

A FEELING OF HELPLESSNESS

Notice that the Israelites and disciples had a feeling of helplessness. And so do we. We, too, often have the grasshopper mentality. We think that the giants in the land are going to destroy us as we meet them. All kinds of giants loom before us, and we feel so helpless before their power. Some have become fearful, negative, cynical and pessimistic. What can we do against the might of the world powers when we seem so small and insignificant? We feel helpless because we forget the power of God. We think only about our own strength. We have forgotten the strength which we draw from God. The Israelites and the disciples alone needed to realize that by themselves they were helpless, but as they drew upon the strength and power of God, he enabled them to meet whatever force lay ahead of them. And so can we.

SELFISHNESS

Selfishness sometimes clouds our vision and causes us to lose sight of the power of God. We focus only upon our own needs. What I do is for my comfort. What I do is for my convenience. Our chief concern becomes what is good for me and makes me healthy and wealthy. Only what satisfies me becomes my chief emphasis. We soon forget about the concerns and needs of others in society and look only at ourselves. Church for some is basically what it can do for them. They ask: "What can I get from the church or out of it?" Will I be given what I want to make me happy and have a good time? There is no sense of a call to service or what I can do for Christ and his church.

A psychiatrist advised a woman one day to remove a mirror over her sink and to cut a window there. He said, "You wash your dishes every day, and all you ever do is look at yourself. You never get beyond your own immediate needs. You need to look through a window so you can see life in a wider perspective." Some of us never get beyond our own needs, and negativism takes over our perspective, because we see life only from our selfish needs and not from the wider angle of others in society being included in the picture.

UNBELIEF

A major reason that we lose a sense of the vision of God is because of unbelief. The Israelites began to see their faith grow weak as they thought about the giants before them. The disciples were not able to perform a miracle, Jesus said, because their faith was too weak. We know something about our own faith seeming to dissipate on occasions, don't we? Sometimes our own faith appears to disappear in the midst of crises, difficulties, and problems, because they seem overwhelming and we do not know where to turn.

In the small book, *Children's Letters to God*, one of the children wrote:

Dear Mr. God,

How do you feel about people who don't believe in you? Somebody else wants to know.

A friend, Neil

God, how do you feel about people who don't believe in you? Especially people who claim to believe in you? What do you think about people, God, when they get in the crises of life where they are experiencing suffering, pain, and difficulties and they find it hard to believe? When the whole world seems to be crashing around us, God, how do you feel about us? God, of course, knows that we human beings are very weak. Before we are too hard on the Israelites, remember they had been slaves in Egypt and had wandered in that wilderness for forty years while they were searching, groping and hoping for the Promised Land. Sometimes our faith, like theirs, is too small.

THE SMALLEST FAITH IS TRANSFORMING

But notice the supreme lesson in these stories is this: Even the smallest amount of faith is transforming. The smallest amount of faith is transforming in the lives of individuals. Jesus said to his disciples: "If you have faith as a grain of mustard seed, you can remove mountains." The mustard seed is a very tiny seed. The seeds look almost like pepper. They are so tiny. Jesus drew his image from the tiniest thing known to the people in that part of the world. "If you have the tiniest speck of faith," Jesus declared, "you have got possibilities of removing gigantic obstacles." "Mountain" was a Jewish metaphor for difficulty. The image was not to be taken literally. If you are going to sit down someplace one day and say, "I'll see if I've got enough faith to remove that mountain across the road from my house" then, you have missed the point of this image. For ancient Jewish people, a mountain was symbolic of great difficulties. If you have the smallest amount of faith, you have the assurance that God will help you meet that difficulty.

Now hear this. Faith has moved mountains in the past. Faith has removed kings. It has transformed empires. Faith has changed pagan culture. Faith has changed individuals. Faith has overcome mountains of greed, prejudice, selfishness, hostility, drunkenness, and laziness. Faith has removed all kinds of mountains in the past, and faith has also built churches, hospitals, universities, children's homes, and other creative agencies down through the centuries to help individuals live a better life. Faith has moved mountains, and faith has also built mountains of goodness in many places.

When we have even a small seed of faith, God begins to cut the giants down to size. If we live with the grasshopper approach to life, everything seems gigantic, but, when we have a small amount of faith, it begins to give us a new perspective on the giant difficulties which loom before us. We know we do not face them alone. We face our giants with the assurance of the power, presence and strength of God to enable us to meet them. "This is the victory that overcomes the world." The scriptures say, "Even our faith." Faith brings alive the power of Christ within us to enable us to face giants. Its transforming power, even as a speck, makes a great difference.

Although the disciples could not cure the young boy down in the valley below the mountain, later they were able to perform miracles in the name of Christ. As Peter and the other disciples went forth to minister, they did have healing powers through the presence of Christ. They did cure people. The same disciples, who did not have enough faith to heal before the resurrection, went forth after the resurrection width a great faith, and they transformed the world and turned it upside down in the name of Jesus Christ. You know that in your own life there have been instances in which you have felt the presence of God. You may have reached out with only a tiny speck of faith, and today you can affirm the difference it has made. "O Lord," the father said in the valley, "I believe, help thou my unbelief." And we make the same cry! Even a tiny bit of belief is sufficient to transform the mountains that are blocking our paths. Let's believe, so Christ can do his work through us.

We have all read stories about individuals who were caught in some traumatic situation. A father, for example, discovers his young son is trapped under a car and he reaches down and literally lifts the car off the child. The child is pulled out safely, and later the father tries to lift the car and he cannot budge it. How does that happen? Where does he get that strength? We don't know for sure. We are told by experts that individuals sometimes are able to get an enormous surge of hidden physical strength in a crisis, which they did not know they had. They draw upon latent strength to do an impossible feat in a sudden moment. These instances indicate the tremendous resources which we have within our body, mind, and spirit which are almost never tapped. How can we draw them forth from the hidden chambers of our inner life? Don't we wish we knew how we could do it? But isn't a part of\what Christ is telling us here that we begin to draw on this hidden power with a tiny seed of faith? That seed is the secret of bringing forth the powers within us.

When I walk with people during the crises of their lives, it is so tragic to witness those who have nothing to lean back upon because they have made no preparation in good days to experience the power of God in their lives. They have no real experience of faith to sustain them. The tiny seed of faith could enable them to meet the great giants that will confront them along life's paths. Our faith can make the difference even if it is small.

OUR ATTITUDE AFFECTS US

When I have observed people in the midst of a crisis, the thing that I have learned which has made all the difference to these persons is their attitude, call it faith or vision. A person's attitude makes all of the difference in the world in how individuals confront these crises. You may not be able to change the circumstances of your life but your attitude can prevent the circumstances from changing you. That makes a radical difference. Sometimes the simplest task without a vision can seem an impossible drudgery. But when there is vision – a different attitude – the hardest task can be done with ease.

Before Lou Holtz went to coach at Notre Dame, he was coach for several years at the University of Minnesota. The team had a record of seventeen straight losses. They had, lost every game by an average score of 47 to 13. Eighteen months later in 1985, Holtz took his team to the Independence Bowl. "It wasn't because of the coach," Holtz said. "It was because of their attitude."[36] Whether it is football, work, or religion, one's attitude in a situation makes a radical difference. What is your attitude toward your problems and difficulties? Attitude is another way of speaking about vision.

THE IMPORTANCE OF VISION

It was vision that motivated Columbus to sail across an unknown ocean-to search for a new world. It was vision that inspired Henry Ford to invent a horseless carriage. It was vision that animated Alexander Graham Bell to believe that persons could talk over a wire. It was vision that inspired the Wright Brothers to believe that human beings could fly. It was vision that heartened Von Braun to believe that it was possible for men and women to go to the moon.

---

36 John Hillkirk and Gary Jacobson, "Count On Me," *USA Weekend* (September 21-23, 1990).

It is vision that inspires poets and musicians, writers and artists, scientists and entrepreneurs, inventors and explorers, athletes and business persons. These people have a sense of call to something beyond what they are now. They have a pull, nudge, whisper, urge, drive, quest, longing, dissatisfaction or compulsion. There is something within that says there is more yet for them to be. They realize that they have not arrived.

What would religion be without vision? Abraham followed God's call in quest of a city without foundations. Moses followed God across a wilderness for forty years, believing that a promised land could become a reality. David had a vision of a united nation, and he brought to Israel the longest reign of peace that they ever experienced. Isaiah had a vision in the temple of God's presence high and lifted up. Jesus, our Lord, had a vision that the kingdom of God could be a reality. Paul had a vision that the gospel was not restricted to the Jewish people but was for persons of all races. Vision led David Livingston to go to Africa; Lottie Moon to go to China; Albert Schweitzer to go to Lambarene; Mother Teresa to go to India. Vision enables us to sense God's pull within us to be more than we have yet become or to serve in a special way.

The demands which come to us from Jesus about our faith seem to be unattainable. He has told us that we are supposed to love our enemies. Who among us really loves our enemies as we should? He instructed us "to do unto others as we would have them do unto us." Who among us does that completely? He commanded us to love our neighbors. Who among us really loves our neighbor fully? We have been challenged by Christ to be his servants in the world. Who among us is really totally serving? Jesus has told us to seek first the Kingdom of God and everything else will be added unto us." Who among us truly seeks first the Kingdom of God? Jesus has declared that we are to be perfect as our heavenly Father is. Who among is completely perfect?

These goals seem unattainable, and, yet, Jesus Christ has lifted them before us to challenge us as we follow him. We may begin with the smallest kind of faith, but we continue, then, to move toward the very highest that we can be, by God's grace and not the least, or the most unworthy. We are challenged to reach for the highest, the farthest, and for the greatest possibilities of what we can be. We may fall short, but we do not settle for the lowest goal we can achieve or a negative goal but for the highest, the best, and the most positive. God summons us to an extraordinary vision.

Michelangelo had a famous student, whom we have already alluded to this morning, whose name was Raphael. One day Michelangelo came to see some of the paintings of Raphael, and noticed a painting on an easel in which all of the figures on it seemed to be so small, faint, and indistinguishable, he took a brush and wrote across the painting, "Amplius! Larger!" He wanted the younger artist to know that if he were going to paint pictures, he had to quit trying to paint everything in its smallest perspective, but to see people, trees, and all of life in its largest possibilities. Our perspective of what God wants for us to be as individuals or as a church is usually too small. Young people, as you step into the future do not dream small dreams but large ones. God is calling us to do great things in his name. Don't settle for a small dream.

Can you remember when your faith was warm, radiant, and vital? Your faith was real and your heart beat with joy. God seemed near and his presence warmed your soul. For some of you, that faith has now grown cold, dull and damp. You no longer see the sunset of God's radiant presence beckoning you toward the horizons of the possibilities which lie before you. This morning let God's Spirit blow the breath of His presence upon the coals of your faith which have become cold and let God fan them once again into a burning, radiant fire of affection. Let your faith come alive again by the warmth of God's presence. Celebrate the wonderful possibilities before this church. Celebrate and be grateful for the outstanding and dedicated staff of ministers and support staff. Celebrate the wonderful Sunday worship and Bible study times and the weekday studies and ministries. This church has a bright future before it and is rich with new possibilities and ministries. Celebrate that! Affirm that! Recapture the vision when God first called you into faith. With renewed vision, you can see the possibilities you have for God in this church, in this community, and maybe even around the world. God calls all of us to heed his vision. Don't lose that high vision. Let God's Spirit motivate and inspire you.

> *Eternal Visionary, Father, Give us a mustard seed faith. We are blind to so much of life and we have not learned to see at all. Forgive us for looking at life in such a negative way. Open our eyes to see the possibilities within us, around us and before us. Most of all may we see the flaming power of your spirit leading us forward through the difficult places of life. Amen.*

14
THANKSGIVING

"WHEN DID YOU LAST EXPRESS THANKS?"

PSALM 100
1 CORINTHIANS 1:4-9
1 THESSALONIANS 5:18

A minister went to his doctor and was advised not to speak for several weeks because he was suffering from what the doctor described as voice fatigue. A minister friend asked him how he felt about not being able to speak. He said, "Well, I don't mind it so much except I have so many things I would really like to shout about." There are an awful lot of feelings at Thanksgiving which arise within us and want to be expressed with a great exuberant voice. Too often, however, many of us have developed voice fatigue when it comes to expressing thanksgiving.

The *first* Thanksgiving in our country was observed in 1619 at the Berkeley Plantation, located on the James River between Williamsburg and Richmond, Virginia. In 1623 William Bradford signed the proclamation which established the "first" *official* Thanksgiving in our country. But it had been observed four years before this official dating. The early settlers and pilgrims found those first years after landing in the new world very difficult. We have all read about the hardships which they underwent. Many of them lost their lives and, from our perspective, the remaining few had very little for which to be grateful. Nevertheless the settlers at Berkeley Plantation in 1619 and a few years later the group of pilgrims gathered together in 1623 and expressed their thanksgiving to God for their lives and the small victory they had won in this new land. It seems strange that 396 years later, with an abundance of blessings, many of us suffer from voice fatigue when it comes to expressing thanksgiving. We simply take our blessings for granted. We somehow assume that all that we have has always been and always will be. So, many do not really bother with expressing gratitude to anyone.

INGRATITUDE IS TOO COMMON TODAY

Unfortunately, ingratitude almost seems to be a part of our culture itself today. It has deep roots. Over a hundred years ago off Lake Michigan, on a freezing winter day, a ship sank near Evanston, Illinois. Some students from Northwestern University swam through the cold water to rescue the people who were drowning. One young man rescued seventeen people. He swam back and forth repeatedly through the icy water until they were all safe. He spent so much time in the freezing water that he came down with an incurable illness which left him an invalid for life.

When someone was talking to this young man later, they asked him if he regretted what he had done. "No, I do not regret what I did," he said. "I think I have done the very best that I could under the circumstances. But the one thing that I cannot understand is this: Of the seventeen people whose lives I saved that day, not a single one of them has ever come to see me. Not one has ever written me a thank you note, nor expressed appreciation in any way at all, or offered any help to me during my illness - not a single one."

We Take Too Much for Granted

Too often we simply accept what is done for us without verbalizing any kind of expression of appreciation. Many assume that others are simply supposed to do those things for us, because that is their job. They are parents; they are teachers; they are merely fulfilling their functions. We take so much for granted.

Many never expect to express appreciation, but they can express complaints if everything is not just right! Complaints and gripes quickly rush to our mouths to be expressed. A man had worked hard at his job all day. He had a job where he had to stand on his feet all day. He got on the bus to go home one afternoon and he really felt weary and tired. The bus was crowded but he found a seat. An older woman got on later and he got up and gave her his seat. After she sat down he looked at her and said: "Beg your pardon, did you say something?" She replied: "No, I didn't say anything." He said, "Oh, I thought you said 'thank you,' excuse me." Isn't it amazing how difficult it is for the words "thank you" to come to our lips, whereas complaints can come rushing forward like storm troopers.

Thanksgiving: A Holy Day

Thanksgiving is a very distinctive American holiday, and I guess it is good that we have one day that we set aside to remind us to be thankful because if we didn't have that one day, I wonder sometimes, when some of us would ever get around to expressing thanksgiving. Any time we use the word holiday, it should remind us of its derivation, which is "holy day." Thanksgiving should be a reminder to us that every day ought to be a day of thanksgiving. The Psalms are filled with expression of gratitude to God. "I will enter his courts with Thanksgiving." "I will sing unto the Lord songs of Thanksgiving." "1 will praise the Lord." "Bless the Lord, 0 my soul, and forget not all his benefits." The Psalmists were constantly praising God for his bounty and blessings. The Apostle Paul wrote to the Corinthian and Thessalonian churches and expressed his thanksgiving to God for them and for the gifts which God had given them. He was thankful for them and the gifts he had seen among them.

WHEN DID YOU LAST EXPRESS THANKS?

It is awful easy, it seems, to receive so much and still have a difficult time expressing gratitude. We take so much for granted. When was the last time you expressed thanks to God because you can think? It has not been too recently, I expect. We simply take the fact that we can think, that we can solve problems; that we can look at something and arrive at a solution, for granted.

I know a middle-aged attorney who developed a disease that slowly took away his ability to recall and he had to give up his practice because he could no longer think properly. He had one of the finest practices in the city but he could no longer remember where he was. His physical body was perfectly healthy but his mind was slowly going. When he would go to the Y to exercise, he might see you and know that he was supposed to know you but he could not recall your name. He might say hello to you and then in a moment speak to you again because he could not remember from one moment to the next who you were or that he had already spoken. When was the last time you thanked God for your ability to think?

When was the last time you thanked God that you can see? We take our sight for granted. My brother, who recently had a detached retina and other eye problems, reminded me of the difficulty he was having in seeing. We take our eyes for granted until we cannot see. When was the last time you expressed thanksgiving for your hearing? Several years ago, I lost partial hearing in one of my ears. Thankfully, I regained my hearing in that ear several weeks later. Since that time, I have always been much more appreciative and understanding of people who have difficulty in hearing. When was the last time you expressed thanksgiving for your ability to hear?

When was the last time you simply thanked God that your body functions properly? In the hospital recently, someone complained to me about a problem that they were having with their bodily functions. We take all of these things for granted and never express thanksgiving to God for them. We just assume that everything will always work until it no longer does. We take for granted the food on our table, the clothes we wear, and the homes we live in, and the job we have. All of these we simply take for granted.

When was the last time you thanked God that we have a church building? Most people usually take their church building for granted. Others before us may have sacrificed that we could worship in this special place today. Surely we ought to express a sense of gratitude for this house of worship. When was the last time you expressed thanksgiving to God for your parents, or children, your wife, or your husband, or our friends? We take them for granted until we can no longer express thanksgiving to them because they are no longer here. Death or distance may have removed them from us. Have you ever thanked God for the person who first led you into your spiritual awareness of God? Have you expressed thanks for the person who introduced you to God and to Jesus Christ? Have you expressed thanks for those who taught you about right and wrong and guided you to seek high moral values in life? Have you ever paused to thank God for your parents, your Sunday School teachers, your ministers, grandparents, or whoever were the first ones who led you to God?

There is an old legend that states that God once sent two angels down to earth. One was to gather a basket filled with petitions, all of the requests which people were asking of God. The other angel was to collect a basket filled with thanksgivings from the people. The angel who returned with the basket of requests could hardly carry it because it was so heavy. But the one with the basket of thanksgiving expressions hardly had any notes in it at all. Why is it so difficult for us to give thanks to God for the great bounty that we have?

In All Things Give Thanks

In writing to the Thessalonians, as recorded in the fifth chapter, the eighteenth verse, Paul admonished, "In all things give thanks to God." Paul didn't say give thanks for all things but in all things. Thanksgiving is not reserved just for the good times. Paul urged his readers to learn the difficult lesson of expressing thanksgiving in the midst of the bad times as well as in the good times. A vital faith makes us want to lift up our voices in praise: "Now thank we all our God." We need to learn to praise God on rainy days as well as on bright sunny days. We need to learn to praise God on dark days as well as on bright days. We need to learn to praise God in days of discouragement as well as in times when we are on the mountaintops filled with enthusiasm. We need to learn to express praise to God in times of illness as well as in times of health. We need to learn to express thanksgiving to God in times of death as well as in times of life. We exclaim with Job: "The Lord gives and the Lord takes away. Blessed be the name of the Lord."

A small book has an interesting title, *The Choice is Always Ours.* It is an anthology of religious writings built around the theme that in every situation in life persons can make a choice. The writers acknowledge that we cannot always control what happens to us but we can control our response to the situation. Our response can make a difference. Do we give in, give up, panic, quit or see what other possibilities there might be. Learning to be grateful can be a meaningful choice in many situations.

We can learn to verbalize praise in all things when we know that nothing can separate us from the presence of God. Whether times are good or bad, God is still present with us to sustain us in everything that happens. Israel learned some of its greatest lessons about God in the wilderness. Paul had suffered greatly for God through persecution, imprisonment, and rejection. But in the midst of all of his suffering, he could still say, "In all things, give thanks unto God."

THANKFULNESS REQUIRES EFFORT AND TEACHING

I am not convinced that we simply become a thankful people without working at it. Thankfulness takes effort. It should be cultivated in our lives and taught to our children and others. We begin by trying to teach our children to learn to be thankful for the small things of life. We teach them to be thankful for their clothes, food, home, parents, church, and all things large and small. They should be taught to verbalize and express thankfulness to others for the things they receive such as gifts, their food, education, toys, etc. Another step in learning thankfulness is to express thanks to God. We learn to express our thanks at mealtime as we praise God for the bounty we have large or small. We remind our children that all gifts ultimately come to us from the hand of a loving God.

An unknown poet has expressed our call to thank God for little things in life.

> Thank you, God, for little things
> that often come our way –
> Things we take for granted
> but don't mention when we pray –
> The unexpected courtesy,
> the thoughtful, kindly deed –
> A hand reached out to help us
> in the time of sudden need –
> Oh, make us more aware, dear God,
> of little daily graces
> That come to us with "sweet surprise"
> from never-dreamed-of places.

THANKFULNESS HELPS US REMEMBER

When we learn to be thankful, it enables us to remember, and when we remember what others have done for us – parents, teachers, and friends – then we remember to be more grateful. When we are more grateful, we are able to express our gratitude more realistically because we remember. We remember that many of our blessings are not really of our own doing so much but are the result of what others have done for us through their time, effort, energy, love, and devotion. Everything has not come to us simply by our own strength.

As we remember, it also makes us more humble because we realize that none of us is totally self-made. We can never be selfish because we have received so much from others in life, and we express our gratitude to God for them. Having received so much from others, we acknowledge our indebtedness to them and express our gratitude for them and the great blessings they have shared with us. Most of all we praise God for his great blessings to us.

CULTIVATE GRATITUDE

We need to cultivate gratitude. William James has reminded us that the fundamental desire of human nature is to be appreciated. It is a longing everyone has. Work at it. Drop notes to others and express your thankfulness. Let us remind our children not to take what we have and are for granted. When is the last time, husbands, you thanked your wife for your meals and the many other things at home she does for you? Too often we take them for granted. When is the last time you expressed appreciation to your wife and didn't just assume that she knew it? Wives, when was the last time you verbalized appreciation to your husband or said, I love you? Children, when have you last expressed your love and appreciation for your parents and, you, parents, for your children? We simply take each other for granted too often.

The parents of a young man killed in one of our wars presented their church with a substantial gift to be used as a memorial for their son. The mother of another soldier learned of the gift and suggested that they also make a contribution.

"Why should we?" the husband asked. "Our son came back home from the war."

"That is precisely the point," the mother exclaimed. "Let's make a gift of thanksgiving because he did come home."

When was the last time you took a moment to express appreciation to somebody who meant a great deal to you? I challenge you this week to drop a note of thanksgiving to somebody – some teacher, a friend, a relative, who has enriched your life. You can never imagine what it may mean to them. After all, you do know what it means to receive one of these kinds of notes. Think what it might mean to someone if you would take the time to address one to them and say: "Hey, what you did for me when I was young or down was helpful. I want you to know it." If not a note, express a word of appreciation verbally to your husband, wife, child, or parent. Let us express our thanksgiving unto God and learn to do so "in all things."

> *Oh All Giving God, we thank you for the great gift you have given to us through Christ Jesus. We express our thanks-giving for the greatest of all gifts - the life we receive through him. Having received so much, teach us to remember to be grateful and to express this gratitude cheerfully in the name of Christ. Amen.*

"It's Hard to Wait for Christmas"

Isaiah 40:27-31
Romans 8:24-25

M uch of our life is spent in waiting. If we do not learn how to live while we wait, we will likely miss much of life. A friend of mine muses: "A lot of living is spent in the meantime." It has never been easy for people to wait in any age. But a flashing sign of our adolescence today is our glaring inability to wait. We are an age of impatience. We want what we want immediately. We want instant gratification. We want results on demand. Actions when requested. In our world today, we do not wait very well. We want everything done instantly. We want news from overseas and even from astronauts in outer space immediately. We want information from those distant places speedily. And often we get it that way by television or the internet. Many today prefer instant tea or instant coffee and minute steaks. They want frozen food made available instantly. Microwaves cook our meals much faster than old-fashioned ovens. We have instant copy makers, fax machines, and many have cell phones, emails and texts to communicate quickly. We have many gadgets and machines to get results quickly or to satisfy our needs immediately. Our lifestyle is one of impatience. We want to be satisfied right now.

WAITING IS A PART OF LIFE

Yet I wonder how realistic that is or has ever been. I recall as a boy that I spent a lot of time waiting. I remember waiting to go to kindergarten, and then waiting until I was old enough to go to first grade. I remember waiting for the school bus. I remember waiting for Saturday so I could go to the old Trenton Theatre and see the "shoot-'em-up" movie. I remember waiting for Christmas Day to arrive and then waiting to go to my grandmother's house for a meal with our extended family, and then waiting to get back home to play with my toys. I recall waiting to go to high school, waiting to go to college, and waiting to go to seminary. Later I remember waiting to get married, waiting for my first child, waiting for my second child and later for my grandchildren.

Much of life is spent waiting. Think about your own life. How much of your life do you spend simply waiting? Reflect on the time you spend at the grocery or the department store waiting at the doctor's or dentist's office. Time is spent waiting for a telephone call from that certain guy or certain girl, or waiting for a call or email from overseas or across the country from a friend or relative, or waiting for the bell to ring at school. "Will this class never end?" you ask yourself. You spend time waiting to go home for Christmas, waiting to get your grades, waiting to graduate, waiting for a job, waiting for somebody else to meet you, waiting for piano lessons to end, waiting for the baby to arrive, waiting for the plane, waiting for the game, play, or concert to begin. We are busy waiting for something. But most of us are not very good at waiting.

J. Barrie Shepherd said that, when he was a very small boy, his father owned a bakery shop. His father would get up very early because he had to knead his dough for the morning rolls which he made the night before. After the dough reached the right consistency, he would drop it in an enormous barrel and then place a piece of yeast on top of the dough and go to bed. Then he would have to get up very early the next day before dawn. The fresh, light dough would have risen to the top of the barrel. He said that the rolls which his father would make from that dough were absolutely delicious. Then America invented a new instant rising substance called "flying dough." His father could sleep later in the morning and prepare the rolls the night before, but Shepherd said that the rolls were never the same again.

Now let me tell you a secret. If you have never tasted a roll made from scratch, or a cake baked from scratch, or a biscuit made from scratch, you haven't really lived! I have been especially blessed to have a wife that can make rolls, cakes and biscuits from scratch. The others that come from a can, the frozen department, or a prepackaged container are not the real things. But that is a part of the sacrifice we make to have everything ready instantly. Convenience or impatience sometimes may cause us to give up some of the better things of life.

THE FRUSTRATION OF WAITING

The prophet Isaiah knew something about the problem of waiting. He was speaking to a people who had been waiting for fifty years to be delivered from their captivity in Babylon. But they had heard no word from God. They longed to go back home to Israel. They wondered where God was. Our text notes first that the children of Israel were filled with frustration and anxiety. They had become faint and weary from waiting. Their long-term burden of suffering and enslavement had affected their mental attitude and they were disappointed and depressed. Our bodily condition often affects our attitude. They had been demoralized from their long years of being away from home in captivity in a foreign land. God's way seemed hidden from them. They cried out and asked: "Where is God? Why doesn't God do something?" They were not concerned whether God was up in the sky or in the stars, but they wanted to know if God was near them in their time of need. They wanted to know if God could do anything to help them in their plight. "Does God care about us?" they asked. In their emotional fatigue and depression, they cried out to God. They were suffering from frustration and anxiety and in the depths of self pity.

You and I understand those kinds of feelings, don't we? There are times when our emotions overcome us because we are weary and faint from physical and mental burdens. Like Israel in Isaiah's day, we want to know where God is. I visited a woman recently who told me she had just talked with her doctor, "I am so tired of hearing him say, 'At your age you have to expect some of your parts to wear out.'" "Why?" she asked. "Why is life that way?" Her body had an affect on her emotions and depression had sunk in. Our body and feelings are tied together. Many of us are frustrated and weary with waiting for something to happen. We have some dream, goal, hope, desire or ideal that we long to realize. But it has not come to pass. Our hope has not been realized or our dream may be unfulfilled, and so we soon become depressed and hit bottom. We feel hopeless or trapped. And we ask, "Is there any word from God?"

The Call for Patience

Isaiah was aware of Israel's frustration and anxiety but note secondly that he encouraged the people to learn to be patient where they were. Even in their waiting, he reminded them that God was present with them. God is working in ways beyond your understanding; Isaiah informs them (v. 28). While they waited, God wanted them to learn to live in the meantime. To a degree, they had done this. They had married, built houses, and had families. They had planted crops and carried on life as best they could while living in captivity. While they waited to return to Israel, they lived in the meantime.

The Gospels record people waiting centuries for Christ to come. We read about Elizabeth waiting to give birth to their son. Simeon and Anna waited to see the anointed One before they died. Mary and Joseph waited for the birth of Jesus. They all waited with expectation and hope. But that did not mean that their wait was easy. We, too, in this Christmas season look for signs again of the coming of the Christ. We wait to celebrate his birth again. Harold Kohn, a minister and naturalist, said that man/woman is the only creature who has really learned much about how to wait. When the amoeba encounters its food, it doesn't wait, it just consumes it. If you want to teach a dog or a cat to wait before they eat, you have a real job on your hands to train them not to eat their food when it is placed before them. If there is no training, there is immediate consumption. And the same is true with many animals in their mating process. There is very little wooing, only instantaneous gratification. But man/woman knows something about wooing and courting and the ability to wait. We plant crops because we have learned to wait for the harvest. We learn how to wait. But not many of us have learned how to wait very effectively.

Waiting requires a great deal of patience. Someone once criticized Leonardo da Vinci because he would stand looking at his canvas of *The Lord's Supper* for hours before he would take a single stroke. People could not understand why he would spend so much time just standing there and looking. He responded by saying: "My most telling strokes come after the longest pauses." His greatest creativity came from his ability to wait until his stroke was clear to him. The best parents, the best teachers are those who know something about patience. Parents and teachers give guidance and knowledge and then wait for the child to absorb it. Education requires the ability to wait and see somebody blossom, develop, grow, and mature. We guide and instruct and then need the ability simply to wait.

Medical doctors have learned to cooperate with waiting. A doctor may remove a tumor or perform surgery and then, after he has finished his or her part, the process of healing must take place. Healing requires waiting. Healing takes time. Healing works on its own. The doctors have done their work. Now time and waiting must take place before their work is complete. Paul reminds us that creation itself is not finished. It is still in process of waiting to be completed. Nature itself waits for its final goal (Romans 8:20-21).

Some years ago when I lost fifty percent of the hearing in one of my ears from a viral infection, my doctor gave me a prescription of rest. He said I needed simply to wait and let my body's natural defenses work on the infection to bring healing. "What kind of prescription was that?" I thought. I want some medicine. Give me something to get rid of this problem." But the doctor's prescription was wait. Wait! But that was not and is not an easy prescription for any of us to take. Waiting can be a hard pill to swallow.

The cartoon character Charlie Brown and Lucy are talking:

Lucy says to Charlie Brown, "Do you know how many great moments in your life you have wasted? Here comes a great moment right now. This is the moment. Bang, it's gone. It's wasted. And you didn't do a thing with it."

Charlie Brown says, "You are not much fun to have around."

And anybody who wants to tell us to live creatively is not somebody we usually want to have around. Nevertheless, we may often need some buzzing bee to remind us to live in the present and stop wasting some of the most precious moments by waiting to live later. We need to learn to live in the time while we wait.

THE ANTICIPATION OF SOMETHING BETTER

Thirdly, notice that one of the reasons Israel may not have been able to live effectively where they were was that they kept anticipating going home. They continued to anticipate something better, something beyond, and returning to something that they did not have. That kind of anticipation is good and bad. Many of us are not able to learn to live right in the meantime because we keep looking down the road. You have heard people say: "Well, if my wife were only different." Or, "If my husband saw things differently or if he were like this…. Or, "If I had different circumstances," or "If I could live differently, or live in another place." So we live in the future and wait for tomorrow. We look to another place and

time or when we graduate or get another job or have more money or the children leave home.

When I have ministered to people who have had heart attacks or bouts with cancer or some other serious illness which threatened their life, they almost universally tell me about the reordering of priorities in their lives. They are no longer looking way down the road. They begin to look more seriously at the present moment. The meantime has become more sacred. Now they ask: "What can I do with the gift of this moment? How can I best live now?" Too many of us look down the road into the future and seek to find life's meaning in a distant direction instead of living in the present.

WAIT WITH HOPE

The writer of our Scripture text offers us a fourth lesson. Isaiah says we have to learn to wait with hope. Waiting can teach us lessons about hope. We can wait or we can wait with hope. We wait with hope in the awareness that the Creator God leads us in ways beyond our ability to understand or grasp. This everlasting God never grows weary or faint. The Apostle Paul writing in the epistle to the Romans reminds us that we wait not as those who have no hope. We wait with expectation. We do not wait for the end to come with inevitability. It will not arrive with a boom and end in despair. We wait with eager anticipation and hope, because we have the assurance that God is in charge of the end of time.

In England the Christmas carolers who used to come by homes singing were called "Waits." The "Waits" shared the Christmas message through music. While we are living in the time of waiting, we need to learn to sing the song of hope. Waiting can teach the Christian how to sing. The Christian cannot be caught up in the despair of the moment, whether there is illness or surgery or sickness or whatever the world conditions are, because we know we wait not without hope, but we wait with a sense of the power and presence of God in our lives to sustain us.

We have experienced his love in Christ, and we know that God loves us and cares for us. We wait in expectation that God will come to meet our need and strengthen us. We wait for God to come anew in our lives in this Christmas season. In a world filled with so much darkness, disease, war, poverty, and injustice, we need to sing songs again of hope, love, peace, joy, forgiveness, and grace. We do not need more prophets of gloom and doom, but those who will deliver songs of encouragement and the possibilities of new beginnings. As Christians, we need to light candles of hope and light in a world filled with too much darkness.

GOD IS CONSTANT

A fifth lesson from our text today is one about trust. Isaiah reminds the people of God's faithfulness and constancy. God is from everlasting to everlasting. God is not a God who grows weary or faint. God is present even when we are weary, tired, depressed and beaten down by difficult circumstances or events. God is ever present. "Have you not known, have you not heard?" Isaiah asked Israel. Have you not known what kind of God we worship? We sometimes assume that faith precedes knowledge. Paul stated, "I know whom I have believed." But sometimes knowledge about God precedes faith. That was what Isaiah was reminding Israel here. Remember that the Lord is an everlasting God. God is the creator of the world. You can never understand the greatness of God nor fathom God's understanding. Isaiah was reminding them of some great truths about God to help them recall or stimulate their faith. Their concept of God was too small.

The basic meaning of the word "wait" comes from a Hebrew word which means "to wind or twist" like a rope or the fibers in a spider's web. "To wait upon the Lord" is to let God become your lifeline, to let God be your cord of escape and to find your strength in God. This concept of "waiting" is not passively doing nothing. It is waiting eagerly like a farmer who waits for crops from seeds he has planted. It is waiting linked with our faith in God knowing that no matter what our troubles or difficulties are, God is always present to sustain us.

Have you ever read or heard how an eagle builds her nest? The eagle makes a nest first with thorns and then places wool or other soft items over the thorns. Then the eagle lays her eggs. When the small eaglets are hatched, they live in the soft nest and are fed for awhile. When it is time for the little eagles to fly, the old eagle removes the soft wool from the thorns in her nest with her talons and exposes the sharp thorns to the eaglets. The nest is very uncomfortable and pricks them. They have to fly out of the nest because the thorns cut them. The young eaglets fly with very weak wings at first. The giant eagle comes under the eaglets and lets the small bird land on his or her wings and bears them up and helps them fly. When the thorns of troubles, difficulties and burdens seem to pierce us that doesn't mean God is not present. God is with us and is seeking to bear us up under the wings of divine grace. We lean upon God knowing that we can feel God's presence and power in our weakness. God will bear us up.

STRENGTH TO ENDURE

Lastly our text reminds us about endurance. Isaiah states that we will "renew our strength" when we wait upon God. The words "renew your strength" are really more accurately translated that we will find "an unfailing strength or resource from God." You will find a strong resource that reaches beyond your own resources and strength. This renewal comes from God's strength, not your own. Here is a new kind of strength. It is from God. This strength will give you the power to endure. Paul reminds us, "If we hope for something we do not yet see, then, in waiting for it, we show our endurance" (Romans 8:25).

Isaiah depicts a graduated or progression of faith. We are not always at the same stage in our faith. Sometimes we have faith like wings. By faith, we can lift ourselves up and fly to great heights. Many of the children of Israel wanted those wings to fly away and escape their bondage. Faith on this level gives us elevation and vision. At other times, by faith we are running. We may be running to avoid our difficulties and trials; running to sustain ourselves in the stresses and strains of living. But most of the time we are walking by faith. This is the faith of our ordinary days, regular rounds, and the steady pace of simply enduring. Much of life is plodding, not running or flying. The greatest work may be done in ordinary, routine ways by teachers, doctors, lawyers, carpenters, secretaries, store clerks, farmers and millions of folks. This is the steady pace of individuals who work faithfully at their routine task again and again, day after day. In our daily work, we walk by faith that God is ever present with us.

In this Advent/Christmas season, let me encourage you again to learn how to wait. Now I know we don't want to do that. We think actions are always the answer and that waiting is a weakness. Action seems stronger. But actions may not be the answer. We sometimes say, "Leave waiting to monks, weaklings and mystics. Give me action." But is it not possible that the greatest source of strength may come to us in waiting? There is a time to wait and a time to act." Knowing the right moment, discerning the time, is not always easy. But try we must.

So then do not give way to despair, difficulties, depressions or whatever those low moments bear. You wait with hope and confidence, because you know that God is present to bear you up. In this Advent season that is the good news. There is good news of great joy. God has come into the world and we have seen his love. As we wait to celebrate Christmas again, remember that God loves you, sustains you and will never abandon you. The birth of Jesus Christ reminds us that God loves us and is present to us in a very special way.

Years ago when our children were preschoolers, we used to drive to church past a manger scene. Each Sunday our children would comment on that manger scene. It was a typical manger scene with shepherds, angels, and the small manger with the Christ child in it. The scene was on the lawn of another church. After Christmas was over, we drove past the church one day and our son, Bill, looked up and said: "They have put the Lord Jesus away until next Christmas."

For some of us we will place the Christmas decorations on the tree and we will get ready for Christmas. After Christmas is over, we will put them away for next Christmas, and we may never have experienced the Christ of Christmas at all. Let us wait for God's presence to come. Let us wait with the sense of the power of God's coming, and with the assurance that in our waiting God is present. We wait with assurance and hope that God has come and is coming anew within our lives to draw us closer to God's self. May your Christmas expectation be fulfilled in the strong sense of the presence of Christ in this Christmas season. May the Lord Jesus not be put away for another year but be a present reality with each of us each day of the new year.

Sometimes at Christmas season we can come aglow with the wonder of Christ but then during the rest of the year we don't really seem to sense much excitement about our faith. My prayer for you and for me in this Christmas season is that we will learn to wait for God and in our waiting sense God's presence sustaining us. It's hard to wait. But remember, bind yourself to God. In that kind of waiting, you find real strength.

Oh Lord God, strengthen us to wait upon You with courage and faith. Amen.

"THE CHRISTMAS SURPRISE"

MICAH 2:13
LUKE 2:1-7

S everal years ago in one of my former churches, the Minister of Music was talking with the three, four, and five year old pre-school choir as they were excitingly awaiting the coming of Christmas. She asked the children, "What does Christmas mean to you?" As you can imagine, she received various responses. Then she said, with a sparkle in her eye, that one of the children gave a description which she liked best of all. "Christmas is a day of surprises," he declared. I like that. Christmas is a day of surprises. Indeed, it has been, and still is in many ways.

CHRISTMAS BEGAN IN A SURPRISING WAY

Christmas was a day that was surprising in its very beginning. Mary was surprised when she received the word that she would be the one to bear the Christ-child. Her cousin Elizabeth was surprised to hear that she would bear the forerunner of the Messiah. Simeon and Anna were surprised when they actually saw the Anointed One. God surprised people in the way that He came into the world. The surprise was so overwhelming that few were really prepared or ready for the way the Christ-child was born.

Christmas is indeed a day of surprises. It was surprising the way that God let humanity know where He was and who He was. What greater surprise could there be than that the Messiah would be born in a manger? The people did not anticipate that nor look for it. Many of them thought that the Messiah would come with some great military or social power to overthrow the political government. Many had anticipated that his arrival would come with military power. God surprised them by not coming in the expected way.

God Comes in Surprising Ways and Places

God has always come in surprising ways and in surprising places. Moses was startled to encounter God in a burning bush. Jacob wrestled with God on a creek bank and found His presence there. Jonah, fleeing from God's presence, found Him in the sea. Isaiah experienced God high and lifted up in the temple. Jeremiah found God in a potters shop while he was on a walk, and he experienced God's presence later in the pit of despondency. Elijah found God in high moments and in low moments, and especially in "a still small voice." Zacchaeus found God while he was up a tree. Matthew found God while he was busy at his work and Christ came walking by. Paul found a radical, new experience with God while he was on a journey.

God often surprises us in the places where He comes into our lives and the way He confronts us with His presence. Some people are able to meet God and understand Him better because they have prepared themselves by worship, They gather together week after week to meet God. This is good and we should do it. But you and I may be surprised to meet God at home while we are working, at school while we are studying, in a visit to a friend in a hospital bed, or on a walk through the woods. Who knows what place or where we might be surprised by the coming of the presence of God. The world was suddenly surprised in the way that God's son was born.

GOD SURPRISES US WITH A PERSONAL ENCOUNTER

God also surprises us not only in the way that he meets us in unusual places, but he surprises us often with how very personal his presence is. Who would have thought that when God came into the world that he would have come as a baby in a manger? Nothing is more personal than a baby. If you and I had been in charge of bringing God's son into the world, would you or I have selected some remote, obscure village on the other side of the world? Bethlehem seems almost a nothing spot in the scheme of the world situation. Would we have done something more dramatic? Would you or I have selected for the birthplace of God's son a palace of a wealthy king or the home of some person with great notoriety, power or influence? Would we have chosen an unknown peasant woman who was not even married? But God chose that particular personal way to bring his Son into the world,

God surprised us with the personal impact of His love and presence through His son. In the tears of Jesus Christ, we sensed something of the personal concern of God for persons in times of our sorrow. In the tenderness of Jesus, as he reached out to those who were lame, blind, deaf, or hurting, we sensed the compassionate concern of God for all persons. In Jesus reaching out to touch the rejected of society, we sensed the presence of God in His personal concern for all individuals. In the anger that we saw in the face of Jesus when He confronted evil, we sensed the personal judgment of God upon sin and corruption in the world. In Christ, God has become very personal and dear to us and we are able to sense something of what His presence is like. He is not abstract, nor distant but immediate, near and available. The presence and power of God has been made known to us in a personal way through Jesus Christ.

Like you, I enjoy getting Christmas cards from people. I have enjoyed the many that we have received locally and from friends we have known in other places. I suppose that one of the things I like most about Christmas cards, especially if they come from people that we have not seen for awhile, is the personal note that is often on the card. Some word is given to update us on the family or their health, success, or many activities. It is exciting to receive a personal word from a friend. It is always a delight on Christmas day or during the season to receive a telephone call from a friend we have not seen for years. How refreshing to receive his or her Merry Christmas and to learn what he or she has been doing and to share our new experiences.

God became very personal in Jesus Christ. But God has always been personal. God has always been available, and still is. Since God has revealed Himself in the coming of Christ, God can no longer be depicted as remote, distant, unsympathetic, and uncaring. Christmas reminds us of how very personal God is in love toward us. God came into history uniquely in Jesus Christ in a way that was immediate and as personal as human flesh.

THE SURPRISING WONDER OF CHRISTMAS

It is also surprising to sense the wonder of Christmas. Look at the wonder of the birth of the Christ-child. What a marvel it was that God's son was born in a manger to an obscure couple in a remote part of the world. Think of the wonder that the message of the announcement of the birth of the Messiah was given primarily to a few shepherds on the hillsides outside Bethlehem and not, to religious leaders. We marvel at the birth of the Son of God who came into the world through a normal ordinary birth.

THE WONDER OF THE WORDS OF CHRIST

Look also at the wonder of the words of this Christ. Many of his words are words that you and I have memorized and hold dear. They have changed the lives of people down through the centuries. Jesus' words have been so powerful that we say: "Sing them over again to me, wonderful words of life." The words that have come from the Christ are words that guide us. They are words that tell us how to relate more effectively with each other and most especially with God. The words of Jesus tell us how to understand God more clearly, how to be more compassionate, forgiving, and generous. They guide us to find our true self and how to walk humbly with God and live in right relationships with others.

The Wonder of Christ's Works

Notice also the wonder of his works. Jesus not only talked but he reached out and touched those with special needs. We saw within this special One, not only a life filled with words, but works that backed up his very life and his testimony. As he spoke about the love of God, it was demonstrated in what he did and how he acted toward others.

The Wonder of the Cross and Resurrection

Look also at the wonder of his death and the resurrection. It was not death on a cross that brought life to us, because many have died on crosses. But it was the death of this particular man on a cross that brings redemption. It is not death on crosses that brings life, but we receive life through this particular cross because of the One who died there and was raised by God the Father. His life, deeds, and words are a part of the wonder of his Incarnation. There is a marvelous surprise and wonder in what God has done for us at Christmas.

The Transforming Power of Christ's Continues

Many are surprised at how transforming the life of Christ has been and continues to be. In the passage from Micah, the prophet depicted the coming Messiah as One who would break down barriers. "The Breaker is come up before them: They have broken up, and have passed through the gate and are gone out by it: and their king shall pass before them, and the Lord at the head of them" (Micah 2:13). Micah and Isaiah were contemporaries. Both of them spoke of the Messiah who would gather his scattered people together and lead them out of the land of slavery back to their promised home. Many looked for a military king to deliver them from the bonds of Babylonian captivity. They envisioned a king who would set them free from their prison with its high wall and massive gates. With the coming of this One, the gates will open, their chains drop off their arms, and they will follow their king to freedom. In this powerful image of the king who sets his people free from imprisonment, the prophet points to the liberating power that many have experienced through the centuries in Jesus Christ.

There Are Prisons of All Kinds

You and I, in a different way, know something about being in prison because many of us are in prisons of various kinds. We are imprisoned in old habits. We cannot free ourselves from habits that have caused us to walk down wrong paths for years. There are others who are imprisoned by lust, hatred, jealousy, or greed. We are imprisoned by selfishness, materialism, tradition, conformity, fear, failure, the past or fear of the future. Our lives can be imprisoned in so many ways. The word on Christmas day is that Christ is the One who breaks down barriers that imprison us. He has come to set us free. He has opened the door. He has come to show us the way of liberation. He brings transformation through his grace and love.

In Micah's image the king, who has come to set his people free, marches before them through the city. The gates have been thrown open, and the people follow behind their king and captain who leads them to freedom. He shows them the way and leads them along its path. Christ is the way, the truth, and the life. He shows us the way to walk.

Christ Is the Path to God

Christ directs us along the truthful path. He leads us into the meaningful life. He is the king and captain who guides us into the way of the abundant life. Christ is the Path and the Pioneer, who through the centuries, has led men and women into the presence of God. Those who have committed their lives to Christ have experienced the birth from above. In Christ, the Path-maker, they have found a new possibility, a new hope, a new song, a new lift, and a rebirth. When Christ enters a life, it is transformed. People are still surprised to see individuals whose lives have been radically altered for good by the power of Christ.

THE SURPRISING POWER OF A MANGER

We are surprised also at the power that God had in a manger. Who but God would think of expressing His power in a manger? Think about the limitless power of God. Paul says in Philippians: "Have this mind among yourselves, which you have in Christ Jesus, who, though he was in the form of God, did not count equality with God a thing to be grasped, but emptied himself, taking the form of a servant, being born in the likeness of men. And being found in human form he humbled himself and became obedient unto death, even death on a cross" (Philippians 2:5-8).

Here is manger power. It is power that is modest and ordinary as it works among us. Manger power is not coercive but is a power which draws by love. Here we sense that God's grace and method are not force, but they are love and gentleness. This power continues to reach out to touch your life and my life and point us in a new direction. God's hand reaches out, not to handle us roughly, but He touches us and guides us gently and gracefully into a new way in what we can become as His children. We marvel at the manger power because it's not interested so much in quantity and bigness but in quality and individuals. Because of the unpretentious and modest way God's son was born, God's presence was sensed only by some shepherds, and a few wise men who followed a star. We often have the mistaken notion that if we have great crowds in church that we are more godly. But God is often working quietly in individual lives seeking to draw them to Himself. God's work is judged successful not in large numbers of hearers but in dedicated persons who have heard and now live for God.

Down through the centuries, the power of the God, who came into our world through a manger, has continued to reach down and change the world with His quiet power. This manger power has brought great universities and hospitals into existence. Humanitarian organizations of all kinds have emerged because of the impact of his presence and deeds on the lives of people. The transforming power that was in a manger continues its work within our world today. May its power increase.

There is an old story that I think is especially appropriate at Christmas time. It tells about an agnostic who was sitting by his fire on Christmas Eve. He was not very interested in Christmas. He really thought that all of this talk about God coming into the world through a baby was a lot of foolishness. It had been a cold day and heavy snow lay on the ground. The fierce weather made it difficult for the birds to find food. He had thrown some seed near his garage for them to eat. But they seemed somehow attracted by the light shining through his window and the warmth of his fire. They attempted to find a way into the room and would fly into the window pane, bounce off it and fall to the ground.

He went over and turned the light on in his garage, hoping that it would attract them to the grain that he had thrown there. But the birds continued to fly against his window pane. He said to himself: "Those stupid birds, what can I do to help them? I sometimes wish I could become a bird and then maybe I could go out there and communicate with them and show them where the food is."

And then it struck him. His thought had been something of the very message of Christmas itself. "In the beginning was the Word, and the Word was with God, and the Word was God. And the Word became flesh and dwelt among us and we beheld his glory" (John 1:14). And he thought out loud: "Maybe that is why God did come into the world. He had been trying to love us. He had tried to help us just like I wanted to help these birds. But it was only when He came into the world in human form that we could really understand something of His grace, power, and compassion." Slowly he sat down again and reflected anew on what the real meaning of Christmas is.

At this Christmastime, the good news is that God has come in Christ. We may be surprised at the way of His coming. We are often surprised at His transforming power; surprised at how personal it is, and surprised at how it continues to work in the world. But most of all, the greatest surprise for each of us is that God has changed us, and we too are new persons because of this surprising power. Christ has come to release that power in each of us. I pray to God that this is true with you on this Sunday before Christmas.

> *Redeemer God, who has given us your Son on Christmas day; who has surprised us with such wonder and mystery that it is beyond our understanding, we thank you for such grace. God, You have loved us beyond our own understanding, we thank you for that. Enable us in this Christmas season to recommit ourselves more deeply to you as we celebrate again the birth of your Son. Amen.*

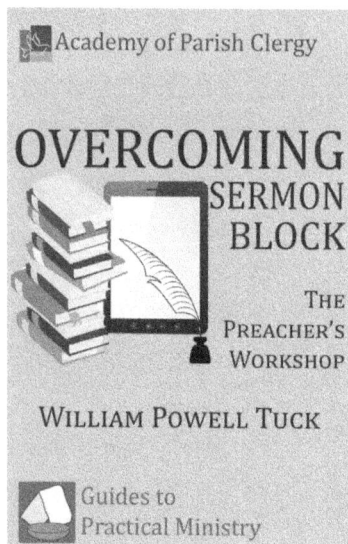

Academy of Parish Clergy

OVERCOMING SERMON BLOCK

THE PREACHER'S WORKSHOP

WILLIAM POWELL TUCK

Guides to Practical Ministry

If I had had this book when I was a seminary student (also many years ago) I would have been a far better preacher than I was. I highly recommend it to others!

John Killinger
Former Professor of Preaching at Vanderbilt Divinity School and Princeton

In these sermons I found the good news of Jesus presented in a fresh, realistic, warm, encouraging, and interesting way.

Fisher Humphreys
Professor of Divinity *Emeritus*
Samford University

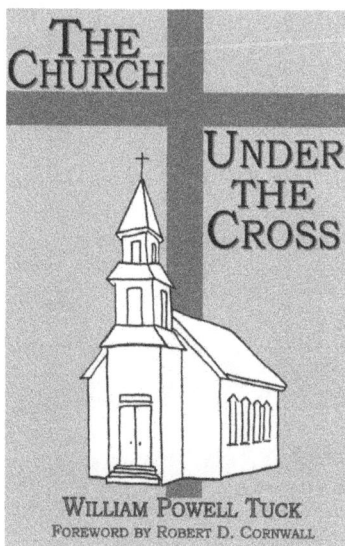

THE CHURCH

UNDER THE CROSS

WILLIAM POWELL TUCK
FOREWORD BY ROBERT D. CORNWALL

MORE FROM ENERGION PUBLICATIONS

Personal Study
Holy Smoke! Unholy Fire	Bob McKibben	$14.99
The Jesus Paradigm	David Alan Black	$17.99
When People Speak for God	Henry Neufeld	$17.99
The Sacred Journey	Chris Surber	$11.99

Christian Living
It's All Greek to Me	David Alan Black	$3.99
Grief: Finding the Candle of Light	Jody Neufeld	$8.99
My Life Story	Becky Lynn Black	$14.99
Crossing the Street	Robert LaRochelle	$16.99
Life as Pilgrimage	David Moffett-Moore	14.99

Bible Study
Learning and Living Scripture	Lentz/Neufeld	$12.99
From Inspiration to Understanding	Edward W. H. Vick	$24.99
Philippians: A Participatory Study Guide	Bruce Epperly	$9.99
Ephesians: A Participatory Study Guide	Robert D. Cornwall	$9.99
Ecclesiastes: A Participatory Study Guide	Russell Meek	$9.99

Theology
Creation in Scripture	Herold Weiss	$12.99
Creation: the Christian Doctrine	Edward W. H. Vick	$12.99
The Politics of Witness	Allan R. Bevere	$9.99
Ultimate Allegiance	Robert D. Cornwall	$9.99
History and Christian Faith	Edward W. H. Vick	$9.99
The Journey to the Undiscovered Country	William Powell Tuck	$9.99
Process Theology	Bruce G. Epperly	$4.99

Ministry
Clergy Table Talk	Kent Ira Groff	$9.99
Overcoming Sermon Block	William Powell Tuck	$12.99

Generous Quantity Discounts Available
Dealer Inquiries Welcome
Energion Publications — P.O. Box 841
Gonzalez, FL 32560
Website: http://energionpubs.com
Phone: (850) 525-3916

www.ingramcontent.com/pod-product-compliance
Lightning Source LLC
Chambersburg PA
CBHW030925090426
42737CB00007B/329